The Poetical Hub

Also by Jack Mitchell

Aphorisms & Poetry

D, or 500 Maxims, Aphorisms, & Reflections
La Rochefoucauld's Reflections, or Moral Opinions and Maxims
The Odyssey of Star Wars: An Epic Poem

Young Adult Novels

The Roman Conspiracy
The Ancient Ocean Blues
Chariots of Gaul

The Poetical Hub

Poems for The Hub
in Common Metre
2021–2024

Jack Mitchell

The Hub
thehub.ca

Printed in Canada
Cover design by Jordan Lunn

ISBN 978-1-998365-67-8

‘At non erunt aeterna quae scripsit’; non erunt fortasse, ille tamen scripsit tamquam essent futura.

‘But the things he wrote won’t last forever’; maybe they won’t, but he wrote them like they would.

Pliny the Younger on Martial
Ep. 3.21.6.

(They did.)

Lucae Smith
subeditori Centri nostri
do dedico

CONTENTS

ACKNOWLEDGEMENTS

First and foremost, I must thank Rudyard Griffiths and Sean Speer, co-founders of *The Hub*, for including poetry in their brave and successful gamble on rational new media. Stuart Thomson, the first editor of *The Hub*, and Harrison Lowman, the second, have been very supportive as well. Ken Whyte has been a great help in the publication of these poems, and Shalomi Ranasinghe did a splendid job in preparing the volume; my warm thanks also to Jordan Lunn for her elegant cover design. I would like to thank my wife, Luba, for enduring many first drafts, often noctural and often self-congratulatory. I would like to thank regular *Hub* readers, especially those who have offered their feedback on the poems, among them Chris Westdal and The Charles Tupper Society. Finally, I would like to thank Luke Smith, Deputy Editor of *The Hub*, for his comradery on this wild ride of poetic composition and for his extraordinary eye for the *Art of the Day* that accompanied the daily poems in *Per Diem*; it's a pleasure to dedicate this volume to him.

ACKNOWLEDGMENTS

PREFACE

The Poetical Hub presents a selection of the nearly 700 poems I've published in *The Hub* since it was launched in April 2021. Most were written in Common Metre originally, and those here that were originally in a different metre have been redone in Common Metre for this volume. A fair proportion have been revised to one degree or another.

The first 250-odd poems here are mostly epigrams, that is, wry or sardonic observations on human character, the modern world, and ordinary life; the latter 125 or so are usually longer and more serious. This division reflects the fact that I was initially brought in to *The Hub* to write a daily short poem for the weekday newsletter, shifting in the summer of 2023 to a weekly longer poem on Saturdays.

Epigram was among the dominant genres of antiquity: the walls of Pompeii feature several originals by ordinary people, and Martial, king of Roman epigrammatists, tells us (11.1) that his book was almost as popular as chariot-racing, which is saying something. It is a genre of many moods, drawing from the stern advice of Theognis (6th C BC) and the laments of epitaph, from the malicious attacks of Archilochus, from the wit of Callimachus and Catullus. It reached its apogee in the 1561 extant epigrams by Martial (c. 100 AD), a number of which are translated or adapted here, especially in Book I. In the longer lyric poems, my chief model has been Horace, my lifelong favourite after Homer.

I am truly grateful to *The Hub* for including my poetry in its effort to revitalise Canadian political discourse: first, for the opportunity to add my oblique observations to its discussions of public policy and modern life; second, for the huge audience thus furnished to my verse; third, for the opportunity to improve my command of rhyme, which I had avoided in my epic poems *The Plains of Abraham* and *The Odyssey of Star Wars*. The challenge of meeting first a daily and then a weekly poetical deadline for four years straight has been highly beneficial to my craft; it also gave me the confidence to base the poems firmly on ideas and arguments rather than on subjective impressions and emotions, a well that soon runs dry. The result is somewhat different from the mainstream poetry of the last hundred years, and I hope it will not only amuse readers but inspire younger poets to explore the range of those poetic genres – epigram and philosophical lyric but also didactic and historical and cosmological poetry – the appeal of which is primarily intellectual and rational rather than sensual. There remain many meadows atop Parnassus waiting for rediscovery.

My work at *The Hub* is ongoing, and I invite readers to subscribe and catch my weekly poem along with *The Hub's* regular political, social, and cultural commentary at https://thehub.ca/.

BOOK I

Epigrams on Human Character

1.

Unpublished

Fly off now, little book, to seek
  A reader with a brain,
Then bring him back inside your beak
  As proof the world's gone sane.

Noah and the dove.

2.

2 June 2021

The vices that we can't correct
  We hardly see as vices:
For them in fact we crave respect:
  Respect, we find, suffices.

3.

19 Aug. 2022

You praise our intellect sublime,
  Our charity, our grace;
Before you preach, perhaps take time
  To meet the human race.

4.

16 Apr. 2021

I can't complain if I provoke
The censor's iron hand
If I'm found guilty of a joke
That censors understand.

Adapted from Karl Kraus: *Satiren, die der Zensor versteht, werden mit Recht verboten* (*Pro Domo et Mundo*: III).

5.

13 Apr. 2021

Genius conceives, attempts, persists
'Til somehow it prevails;
Madness conceives, attempts, insists,
And, still insisting, fails.

6.

3 May 2021

You argue well that less is more,
But, Bob, I must confess,
I hope you'll pause for breath before
You prove that more is less.

7.

15 Apr. 2021

I'd rather be misunderstood,
I'd rather lose control,
Than find I'd gotten far too good
At laying bare my soul.

8.

5 May 2021

By living, Bob, we learn to die,
For that's the Lot of Men:
To wander looking for a why
And find it's just a when.

9.

26 Apr. 2021

He scowls, he shrugs, he rolls his eyes
At flattery's empty phrase,
Preferring (or so we surmise)
A truer paean's praise.

10.

2 July 2021

It's only in the desert waste,
When steps begin to totter,
We learn the most delightful taste
Lies in a drop of water.

11.

13 May 2021

Although your ask was tiny, Grace,
They laughed you out the door;
Here's my advice: next time save face
By asking ten times more.

Adapted from Martial 11.68: *Parva rogas magnos; sed non dant haec quoque magni. / Ut pudeat levius, tu, Matho, magna roga.*

12.

23 July 2021

At first I found you boring, Drew:
That's fine: a man must live;
But then you found me boring too,
And that I can't forgive.

Adapted from La Rochefoucauld #304: *Nous pardonnons souvent à ceux qui nous ennuient, mais nous ne pouvons pardonner à ceux que nous ennuyons.*

13.

7 May 2021

You give me nothing while alive:
  Your will, you say, must do;
What gift do you imagine, Clive,
  I'm looking forward to?

Adapted from Martial 11.67: *Nil mihi das vivus; dicis post fata daturum. / Si non es stultus, scis, Maro, quid cupiam.*

14.

20 May 2021

The gods, on bright Olympus, set
  The price of wisdom high;
And we grow wise when we forget
  To ask the reason why.

15.

10 May 2021

Gaze not too deep into the bleak
  Void of eternity,
Gaze not, for what true pilgrims seek
  No man can ever see.

On Nietzsche's injunction that we "not gaze too long into the void" (*Beyond Good and Evil* #146).

16.

28 May 2021

By turns they rise to give a speech:
  Don't say you're not impressed
How wrong about himself is each,
  How right about the rest.

On Parliament.

17.

14 May 2021

They say he's writing quite the screed,
He's got me in his sights;
But what no reader's eye will read
A writer hardly writes.

Adapted from Martial 3.9: *Versiculos in me narratur scribere Cinna: / Non scribit, cuius carmina nemo legit.*

18.

21 May 2021

As Goethe said, a man is never
Riper for ridicule
Than when a man is very clever
Yet still remains a fool.

Adapted from Goethe, *Maximen und Reflexionen* #223: *Einem Klugen widerfährt keine geringe Torheit.*

19.

4 Aug. 2021

I know you've oftentimes complained
That Billy smells like beer;
The fault is yours, I've ascertained,
For talking in his ear.

Adapted from Martial 3.28: *Auriculam Mario graviter miraris olere. / Tu facis hoc: garris, Nestor, in auriculam.*

20.

31 May 2021

By discipline we seek to soothe
The rattle of the mind;
By discipline we grow more smooth
And with the world aligned.

Adapted from Patanjali, *Yoga Sutras* 2–4: योगश्चत्तितवृत्तनिरिोधः / तदा द्रष्टुः स्वरूपे ऽवस्थानम् / वृत्तसारूप्यमतिरत्र

21.

5 Aug. 2021

Objectively I must condemn
  Autobiography:
That genre mostly turns on them,
  So seldom, Bob, on me.

22.

8 Oct. 2021

You're smarter than you look: you choose
  To try and tie the knot
With Priscus: what, can he refuse?
  He's smarter than I thought.

Adapted from Martial 9.10: *Nubere vis Prisco: non miror, Paula; sapisti. / Ducere te non vult Priscus: et ille sapit.*

23.

12 Aug. 2021

That man is a celebrity,
  With brains as well as fame;
Yet how much brainier he'd be
  If no one knew his name!

Adapted from Nietzsche *Daybreak* 282: *Diese Frau ist schön und klug: ach, wie viel klüger aber würde sie geworden sein, wenn sie nicht schön wäre!*

24.

13 Aug. 2021

You see me walking down the street,
  You wave: "What's up?" you say —
Whether it's once a week we meet
  Or twenty times a day,

Five times an hour! You must confess
  This much at least is true:
Whatever's up on my side, Les,
  There's nothing up with you.

Adapted from Martial 2.67: *Occurris quocumque loco mihi, Postume, clamas / protinus et prima est haec tua vox 'Quid agis?' / Hoc, si me decies una conveneris hora, / dicis: habes puto tu, Postume, nil quod agas.*

25.

11 Aug. 2021

The expert, newly crowned, struts past,
  Advancing by degrees
To knowledge, 'til he sheds at last
  His air of expertise.

Adapted from the *Hagakure* Chapter 2 (W. S. Wilson transl.): *A person who knows but a little will put on an air of knowledge. This is a matter of inexperience. When someone knows something well, it will not be seen in his manner.*

26.

12 July 2021

"It's nothing, really": so you say,
  While staring at your shoes;
Well, if it's nothing, ask away
  And nothing I'll refuse.

Adapted from Martial 3.61: *Esse nihil dicis quidquid petis, inprobe Cinna: / si nil, Cinna, petis, nil tibi, Cinna, nego.*

27.

16 June 2021

Apply yourself to study, Ern,
  While you're still in your prime,
For only study lets us learn
  What isn't worth our time.

28.

1 June 2021

You wonder, Egbert, who's to blame
  Your teachings didn't last?
Perhaps because you didn't aim
  One day to be surpassed.

29.

15 June 2021

He'll march on Rome, and either way
  Win infinite renown:
Over the trembling world hold sway,
  Or die a bloody clown.

30.

15 July 2021

A thing we've never understood,
  A thing we've never known
We cannot judge as bad or good
  Nor ever call our own.

Adapted from Goethe, *Kunst und Altertum* 3.1 (1821): *Was man nicht versteht, besitzt man nicht.*

31.

28 July 2021

Roger, I've pondered once or twice
  A mystery unsurpassed:
How far you are from being nice
  Although you've finished last.

With reference to the proverb that 'Nice guys finish last.'

32.

7 July 2021

If love's as pricy as you say,
  What miser can afford
To live without it and so pay
  The price of being bored?

33.

30 Aug. 2021

This politician wows the crowd:
  They'll get their choice of bribe,
At least so long as he's allowed
  His choice of diatribe.

34.

1 Oct. 2021

Whether I whisper it, my friend,
  Or shout it in your ear,
A truth you'll never comprehend
  I know you'll never hear.

Adapted from Goethe's aphorism, *Es hört doch jeder nur, was er versteht.*

35.

18 Oct. 2021

Toward experience we reach,
  Our childhood left behind:
Experience alone can teach
  An open heart and mind:

For if the mind no longer grows
  In youth or middle age,
The open heart is quick to close
  And shrivel into rage.

36.

4 Oct. 2021

You've seen it all before: this year
  Is just the same. My theory:
You started your august career
  Already pretty weary.

37.

24 Sept. 2021

My cottage at Nomentum, Linus:
  You say it's distant? True!
The point of such a cottage, Linus?
  The distance is from you.

Adapted from Martial 1.38: *Quid mihi reddat ager quaeris, Line, Nomentanus? / Hoc mihi reddit ager: te, Line, non video.*

38.

6 Sept. 2021

They offer only empty praise,
  Empty and faulty too;
But that's the best I get these days,
  So that'll have to do.

39.

5 Nov. 2021

Henderson keeps my book in hand,
  He reads it, he recites:
But when he does it sounds so bland
  I'm giving him the rights.

Adapted from Martial 1.38: *Quem recitas meus est, o Fidentine, libellus: / sed male cum recitas, incipit esse tuus.*

40.

19 Oct. 2021

"The golden mean, the golden mean":
  The zeal that some profess
For moderation is so keen
  It verges on excess.

41.

11 Oct. 2021

They're proud to rush, they'll never see
It takes more strength of will
To let the rush and rumble be
And proudly just sit still.

42.

5 Jan. 2022

You say you're keen to hear my work;
Forgive me if I groan:
I know that, when you say so, Kirk,
You're keen to read your own.

Adapted from Martial 1.63: *Ut recitem tibi nostra rogas epigrammata. Nolo: / non audire, Celer, sed recitare cupis.*

43.

25 Nov. 2021

Defending him, you say that Man
Is foolish more than cruel;
That's no defense: what's crueler than
The cruelty of a fool?

44.

20 Nov. 2021

How hard he worked to earn our love,
How little he'll be missed:
He always wore the velvet glove
Upon the velvet fist.

45.

10 Dec. 2021

Discard a man's opinion 'til
  You sift him through and through;
Discard your own: what lingers, Bill,
  At least belongs to you.

46.

13 Jan. 2022

I hate, I love; I love, I hate;
  Maybe you wonder why:
I cannot say: it's just my fate
  Myself to crucify.

Adapted from Catullus 85 (c. 60 BC): *Odi et amo. Quare id faciam fortasse requiris. / Nescio, sed fieri sentio et excrucior.*

47.

18 Jan. 2022

My lady says she'd never wed
  With anyone but me;
Not if the King of Heaven pled
  For her fidelity;

Aye, so she says, but what is said
  To lovers on a knee
Is carved in breezes overhead
  And printed on the sea.

Adapted from Catullus 70: *Nulli se dicit mulier mea nubere malle / quam mihi, non si se Iuppiter ipse petat. / Dicit: sed mulier cupido quod dicit amanti / in vento et rapida scribere oportet aqua.*

48.

19 Jan. 2022

You sold your friends, you sold your soul,
  Your city, clan, and folk;
You plundered, scammed, extorted, stole—
  How is it, Bob, you're broke?

Adapted from Martial 11.66: *Et delator es et calumniator, / et fraudator es et negotiator, / et fellator es et lanista. Miror / quare non habeas, Vacerra, nummos.*

49.

20 Jan. 2022

In peaceful times a man of war
  Attacks himself: like Ney,
He mounts, he bids the great guns roar,
  Then charges to the fray.

Adapted from Nietzsche, *Beyond Good and Evil 76: Unter friedlichen Umständen fällt der kriegerische Mensch* über *sich selber her.*

50.

21 Apr. 2022

I'm grateful for your sympathy
  But find it rather witty,
Preferring the solemnity
  Of self-provided pity.

51.

19 May 2022

Here lies a man who lived for strife,
  Gone now to meet his Lord;
I hope there is an afterlife:
  He's trouble when he's bored.

52.

22 Nov. 2021

You said it was a slippery slope,
My steep philosophy:
So how do you intend to cope
On one cross-country ski?

53.

6 Apr. 2022

I'm always first to say Hello,
Then wait for your reply;
But if you're always second, Joe,
You get the long Good-bye.

Adapted from Martial 5.47: *Saepe salutatus numquam prior ipse salutas: / sic eris Aeternum, Pontiliane, Vale.*

54.

20 May 2022

Laecania's teeth are white and full,
While Thaïs' teeth are black;
Why? Thaïs' teeth are natural,
Laecania's off the rack.

Adapted from Martial 5.43: *Thaïs habet nigros, niveos Laecania dentes. / Quae ratio est? Emptos haec habet, illa suos.*

55.

28 Jan. 2022

From distant peoples well beyond
The north I've sent you hairs
So you may see how much more blond
Your tresses are than theirs.

Adapted from Martial 5.68: *Arctoa de gente comam tibi, Lesbia, misi, / ut scires quanto sit tua flava magis.* Stylish Roman women often either dyed their hair blond or used blond extensions imported from Scandinavia.

56.

22 Mar. 2022

This man's associates displease,
  His attitude offends;
But, judging by his enemies,
  He'll prove the best of friends.

57.

2 May 2022

He's sacrificed his dignity
  To gratify his chums:
Though not the fool he seemed to be,
  A fool he soon becomes.

58.

13 June 2022

For temperance and sobriety
  Bill's one you'd recommend?
He sounds well qualified to be
  A butler, not a friend.

Adapted from Martial 12.30: *Siccus, sobrius est Aper; quid ad me? / Servum sic ego laudo, non amicum.*

59.

2 June 2022

Would we still strive to cultivate
  The virtues of the wise,
If not for fools who demonstrate
  What vices to despise?

60.

13 May 2022

They call ambitious men uncouth,
  An insult often hurled;
But when ambition serves the truth
  Ambition saves the world.

61.

11 July 2022

You toast me as your heir, good Ben,
  You say it's so exciting;
But I'll be more excited when
  I see your toast in writing.

Adapted from Martial 12.73: *Heredem tibi me, Catulle, dicis. / Non credam, nisi legero, Catulle.*

62.

13 July 2022

He's got Imposter Syndrome? Why?
  You must admit that's odd:
For where's the syndrome when the guy
  Is actually a fraud?

63.

21 June 2022

There's several roads to happiness,
  There's five or six to seek;
But every journey through excess
  To ruin is unique.

64.

5 July 2022

Some work so hard to get ahead,
They fight for every crumb;
But others bait their hooks instead
And let the suckers come.

Adapted from La Bruyère, "Des biens de fortune" 52: *Il n'y a au monde que deux manières de s'élever, ou par sa propre industrie, ou par l'imbécillité des autres.*

65.

18 July 2022

Your braids are long, your beard is blue,
Your creed is vaguely Druid:
You're not exactly Celtic, Stew,
You're more like Celto-fluid.

There was a fad for being 'gender-fluid,' the gender-fluid person often having hair dyed blue or purple and (in the popular imagination) a personal philosophy bordering on the mystical.

66.

29 July 2022

You're undecided, still unsure,
You're neutral, non-aligned;
Your only principle is pure:
You like to change your mind.

67.

30 Aug. 2022

The boss won't raise your salary,
You say you feel betrayed;
But some guys, Bob, could work for free
And still be overpaid.

68.

10 Aug. 2022

You wrap a scarf around your neck
  Before your work premières;
I'll need to use it in a sec
  To wrap around my ears.

Adapted from Martial 4.41: *Quid recitaturus circumdas vellera collo? / Conveniunt nostris auribus ista magis.*

69.

7 Oct. 2022

You praise the art of eloquence,
  You love a good long speech;
But here's the only problem, Spence:
  You practice what you preach.

70.

13 Oct. 2021

He's quite the party animal,
  He's looking pretty wan;
But that's not last night's booze we smell:
  He drank 'til well past dawn.

Adapted from Martial 1.28: *Hesterno fetere mero qui credit Acerram, / fallitur: in lucem semper Acerra bibit.*

71.

24 Aug. 2022

You brag your views are just the same
  Today as yesterday;
Consistency must take the blame
  If few care what you say.

72.

14 Mar. 2023

You cite the guy who cites the guy
Who cites some guy in college;
What cynic, Bob, would dare deny
You're cranking out the knowledge?

73.

18 Oct. 2022

Her new collection is sublime,
The style not uninviting;
Alas, her readers don't have time:
They're all too busy writing.

74.

15 Aug. 2022

You write so many verses, Reid,
There's no time to recite them;
So fans and foes are all agreed
You mustn't cease to write them.

Adapted from Martial 8.20: *Cum facias versus nulla non luce ducenos, / Vare, nihil recitas. Non sapis, atque sapis.*

75.

20 June 2022

I'm grateful, Bob, for all your takes,
I find them quite delightful:
What else besides the contrast makes
My verses seem insightful?

76.

30 Nov. 2022

As no great heavyweight I sing,
  Indeed my verse is light:
For that's the lesson of the ring:
  You have to dance to fight.

77.

8 Aug. 2022

You fret I haven't sent you, Wade,
  My latest book for free;
That fact is that I'm too afraid
  You'd send your book to me.

Adapted from Martial 7.3: *Cur non mitto meos tibi, Pontiliane, libellos? / Ne mihi tu mittas, Pontiliane, tuos.*

78.

9 Aug. 2022

Unless they're dead, no poets seem
  To fully satisfy;
Forgive me if, for such esteem,
  I'm not prepared to die.

Adapted from Martial 8.69: *Miraris veteres, Vacerra, solos / nec laudas nisi mortuos poetas. / Ignoscas petimus, Vacerra: tanti / non est, ut placeam tibi, perire.*

79.

29 Dec. 2022

A poem can sing of lofty bliss,
  A poem can be a bummer,
But all I ask of it is this:
  It shouldn't make me dumber.

80.

14 Oct. 2022

You say your situation's bad,
  You say you're much aggrieved;
And, Bob, if you looked half as sad,
  You might well be believed.

81.

16 Nov. 2022

Yes, quite the labour shortage, Brie:
  Don't mean to be a jerk,
But microeconomically
  You don't do any work.

82.

25 Nov. 2022

The more he labours to astound,
  The more the listener frets:
The more he strives for the profound
  The shallower he gets.

83.

13 Feb. 2023

You're greedy, loud, a fearful slob,
  Incorrigibly lewd;
In certain parts you're famous, Bob,
  For perfect rectitude.

84.

23 Jan. 2023

The Laws of Farce forbid, madame,
   That anyone suggest
You've fallen for a total scam
   'Til you yourself have guessed.

85.

18 Jan. 2023

You're glad the tide is rising, Lou:
   So nature's on your side;
But soon there's something else that you
   Must learn about the tide.

86.

9 Feb. 2023

You dearly love to orate, Geoff:
   Your eloquence is such
As might persuade or charm the deaf;
   The others not so much.

87.

27 Feb. 2023

Your views are most impressive, Finn,
   They've opened many doors:
Your views have helped you fit right in
   And none of them are yours.

88.

5 Dec. 2022

He thinks he's wealthy, this sad slave
Of avarice and greed:
Rich only in new things to crave
And poor in what men need.

89.

23 Mar. 2023

He's got whole houses full of bling,
Stuff piled on piles of stuff:
Why bother owning everything
When nothing is enough?

90.

4 Aug. 2022

This man's good humour has defied
Mortality's grim sickle:
He sees it press against his side
And only feels a tickle.

91.

5 June 2023

You're right, I've had to change my view:
It wasn't easy, Reid;
But after that long talk with you
I feared that we agreed.

96.

10 May 2023

In spite of all my lessons, Dan,
It's happened yet again:
You've let your noble faith in Man
Inflate your faith in men.

97.

3 Aug. 2021

Apollo, once again I vow,
Though many years have passed,
To take the road to Delphi: now
I know myself at last.

On the Delphic injunction to 'know thyself.'

98.

6 Apr. 2023

You like your epigrams obscene,
You point to Martial's stuff:
Indeed your appetite is keen
If Martial ain't enough.

99.

16 Dec. 2021

All Rome agrees my book is grand,
They love it and they quote;
In every pocket, every hand
Are verses that I wrote.

See how the reader pales and stares,
Blushes and gapes and foams:
My own reaction's just like theirs:
At last I like my poems.

Adapted from Martial 6.60: *Laudat, amat, cantat nostros mea Roma libellos, / meque sinus omnes, me manus omnis habet. / Ecce rubet quidam, pallet, stupet, oscitat, odit. / Hoc volo: nunc nobis carmina nostra placent.*

100.

31 May 2022

The reader merely smiles and sighs,
Saying he's not offended;
Dear reader, I apologise:
That's not what I intended.

BOOK II

Epigrams on the Modern World

101.

25 May 2021

You warn the end is coming, Drew:
  We're destined for the chop;
Okay, but why is every new
  Apocalypse a flop?

We wait and wait for bombs and guns
  To blow the place sky high,
Then watch the brash barbarians
  Turn back or pass us by.

There's no denying it's a mystery
  Quite hard to reconcile:
This celebrated end of history
  Is lasting quite a while.

102.

8 Feb. 2023

We used to grumble and deplore
An age so uninspired;
I miss those quiet days before
We got what we desired.

103.

23 Sept. 2021

One observation, Howard, drives
The steel into my nerves:
Whether a nation fails or thrives,
It gets what it deserves.

104.

12 May 2021

A parent does not cease to chide,
To comfort, to entreat;
A patriot does not cease to guide
The nation's clumsy feet.

105.

29 Sept. 2022

Like clockwork, every fifteen years,
Hysteria sets in:
For men would rather shed hot tears
Than wallow in chagrin.

106.

28 Apr. 2021

They labour to beautify
Their fables, though the truth
Is always cruder than a lie,
And always more uncouth.

107.

22 Apr. 2021

Soon these stupidities will shatter
  Like some schismatic church,
The cant and slogans only matter
  In dull-as-dust research.

108.

18 Oct. 2021

He says he's sorry: he'll repent;
  They answer that he's scum;
I knew the guy was innocent
  But not that he was dumb.

109.

27 May 2021

You cursed me in the public square,
  Foolishly, it appears:
Now people think the gods don't care
  Or chuckle at your tears.

110.

29 June 2021

You poor inquisitors, whose shtick
  Must claim that lies are true:
You would not hate the heretic
  Unless you doubted too.

111.

21 Oct. 2021

You force me to respect your god,
  But what if I detect
My new religion is a fraud
  And lose my self-respect?

112.

15 Apr. 2022

Perhaps somewhere beyond our ken
It's safe from falsifiers,
But here the truth's in trouble when
Its guardians are liars.

113.

19 May 2023

You say we'll simply grit our teeth,
The panic will abate;
But what if in our culture, Keith,
The panic is innate?

114.

9 Feb. 2022

Freedom of speech, you say, is lame,
Like freedom to protest;
Indeed, you say, it's all the same,
We'll never be oppressed;

The fact is, Bob, as you explain—
Your theory's pretty hazy—
You'll never go against the grain:
Let's face it, Bob, you're lazy.

115.

18 June 2021

How smugly they instruct the youth
To give their lives and be
Glum martyrs to the deathless truth
Of mediocrity.

116.

18 Nov. 2021

The only problem with God's love
Is this: how very few
Can tell it from the comfort of
A comfortable pew.

A 'comfortable pew' refers to a comfortable station in life.

117.

14 July 2021

They slam the book of history shut
With fury and dismay,
Forgetting they themselves are but
Tomorrow's yesterday.

118.

16 June 2023

You're striving to eradicate
Intolerance, Sinclair;
Too bad you only tolerate
Opinions that you share.

119.

30 Sept. 2023

They barely know the Holocaust,
  It happened in some war;
Though living memory's not quite lost,
  It happened, well, before—

Back in the age of books, of days
  Free of the little screen,
Of conversation, leafy ways,
  And consciences still keen.

Today bad children rule us, Jake,
  Their every word pretend,
The latest tantrum always fake;
  Yet soon their reign will end,

For soon no one will rule, I fear,
  And no one will be ruled,
No one will grumble, no one cheer,
  And no one will be schooled:

Time mixes all, muddles the world,
  My world of yesterday;
The colours of the past are swirled
  Into a dull, dull grey.

120.

8 June 2022

I gripe, I grumble; you respond
  With talk of heaven's bliss;
But what if, in the Great Beyond,
  They're just as dumb as this?

121.

16 May 2023

At history's crimes you stand aghast,
  Its horrors leave you numb;
I'll take th' injustice of the past
  Compared to what's to come.

122.

14 Jan. 2022

Decline is fine, I'm used to it:
  It's what the gods assigned;
For history's sake at least admit
  The gods are seldom kind.

123.

23 Mar. 2022

I know you've always prophesied
  We'd somehow muddle through,
But better worlds than ours have died
  Still thinking that was true.

124.

20 July 2021

The surest symptom of decay
  Is readers who demand
Only to read of symptoms they
  Already understand.

125.

31 Aug. 2022

You say the worst can't happen, Biff,
  We're simply disenchanted;
But what is there to stop it if
  We take the best for granted?

126.

10 Aug. 2021

Oh, he's a citizen indeed,
  A patriot to the bone:
He sometimes thinks his country's need
  Might differ from his own.

127.

10 Nov. 2021

The road to power from online sage,
  From posts to passing laws,
Is longer than from shower to stage
  And rapturous applause.

128.

21 Jan. 2022

The guy who passes on the right,
  Or drives it like a boat,
The guy who sits there at the light —
  Remember that they vote.

129.

8 Mar. 2022

Alone, mere bluntness is his flaw;
En masse, hypocrisy;
So always trust a *bon bourgeois*,
Never the bourgeoisie.

130.

11 May 2022

His rhetoric's hysterical,
He sneers, he stamps, he drools;
If that's an intellectual,
Count me among the fools.

131.

6 May 2022

The masses teeter in suspense
To learn the wise man's view;
It's always a coincidence
He thinks what they think too.

132.

1 June 2022

I'm sorry, Stan, you're so incensed!
The good news is, it seems
That half the foes you rail against
Are merely last month's memes.

A 'meme' was an Internet reference, usually in pictorial form with caption, depicting a general situation or emotion, which users would adapt to comment on a particular situation or emotion.

133.

21 June 2022

Alas, your righteousness can't see
That every man's your brother:
You've merely you've shed one bigotry
To grow yourself another.

134.

1 Mar. 2022

Why is our wintry northern nation
Kinder than overseas?
Just this: though few here fear starvation,
We're all afraid to freeze.

135.

25 Aug. 2022

You're shocked that I deplore your view,
You're only used to Yes:
But, Bob, what I deplore is you,
Whatever you profess.

136.

Unpublished

His conscience swells, his conscience frets,
His conscience often swerves;
No wonder if his conscience gets
On everybody's nerves.

137.

16 Aug. 2022

As curses go, it's quite unique—
  Though not one I'd have picked—
In every book in vain to seek
  A view I can't predict.

138.

1 Aug. 2022

The fact he's sketched the heartless laws
  Of history won't preclude
That someday in those very jaws
  He shall himself be chewed.

139.

7 July 2022

Man isn't hungry for belief,
  He's famished: much I dread
That well before he finds relief
  He'll eat himself instead.

140.

21 July 2022

The market of ideas is where
  Inflation is no joke:
Soon every man's a millionaire
  And everybody's broke.

141.

2 Aug. 2022

You won't revise or overhaul,
  Won't modify your view.
Why not improve it? After all,
  It'd still belong to you.

142.

2 Sept. 2022

Oh, let me shake his saintly hand
  And beg an autograph:
He heard the wisdom of the land
  And managed not to laugh.

143.

7 Dec. 2022

Of course we all appreciate
  A scholar's self-reliance,
But what no one can replicate
  Is something else than science.

On the 'Replication Crisis,' a term for the increasing unreliability of published, but unreproducible, scientific research.

144.

7 Nov. 2022

He's boasting of his GPA
  In 2022?
How better can a youth display
  He hasn't got a clue?

He plans to join the oligarchs,
  Leaves nothing left undone;
Alas, poor lad, he's buying Marks
  In 1921.

On grade inflation and the commercialisation of higher education. The German Mark suffered hyperinflation in 1921.

145.

11 Oct. 2022

You sure dislike reality,
  And, Roger, that's your right;
But don't make it your enemy
  Unless you like to fight.

146.

12 Apr. 2023

Forgive me, Roger, if I fret,
  But something's slightly off:
You're racking up the student debt
  Dressed better than your prof.

147.

9 Nov. 2022

You eat like you're a millionaire,
  You're notably well dressed,
You rage that people just don't care
  How harshly you're oppressed.

148.

24 Nov. 2022

The blood, the boils, the insect horde,
  The frogs that fall like snow;
Just send the law-school midwits, Lord:
  He'll let our people go.

149.

28 Dec. 2022

In this poor minister's defence,
He's not on Twitter, Wyatt:
I don't much mind incompetence
So long as it keeps quiet.

150.

16 Mar. 2023

Among the many springs of hope
There's one he didn't mention:
Just six more years and he'll elope
To Europe with his pension.

151.

13 Mar. 2023

You've held your breath, you're turning blue:
It's most impressive, Gail;
What disappointment, then, that you
Eventually exhale!

152.

28 Nov. 2022

What punishment is there more cruel,
What hotter ring of hell,
Than always to be stuck in school
Forbidden to excel?

153.

10 Mar. 2023

Across the battlefield of truth,
  Toward the hostile lines,
They've launched the crowded ranks of youth
  To clear away the mines.

154.

22 June 2023

He asked us once, he asked us twice,
  We didn't want to pay:
We thought he'd just bring back the mice;
  He piped the kids away.

155.

10 Nov. 2022

You scowl and call the young naïve,
  But that's the charm of youth:
They needn't bother to perceive
  The universal truth.

156.

19 Oct. 2022

What joy to see my son rejects
  The lie of doublethink:
We raised him right if he expects
  That garbage ought to stink.

157.

19 July 2022

To kill a bad idea is not
As hard it appears:
Just make kids chant the thing a lot
And then wait thirteen years.

158.

11 May 2023

The course is fixed, the course is set,
The course cannot be changed;
Be patient while the deck chairs, Brett,
Are bravely rearranged.

159.

1 Nov. 2022

I'm willing, Bob, to make a bet
The age won't last for long,
Since everything is bungled, yet
Nobody's ever wrong.

160.

25 Apr. 2023

You want your foes to shiver, Reid,
To dread your awful name;
But by those lights it's guaranteed
They'll make you do the same.

161.

9 May 2022

A day or two a lie persists,
  Then visibly decays;
But what's conceived in truth exists
  Until the end of days.

162.

17 Jan. 2023

The gabble of democracy
  Provokes me to atone:
It shows a fool's philosophy
  Is too much like my own.

163.

21 Mar. 2023

I guess I'm an elite dead-ender:
  Like old Cambronne declared,
"The Old Guard dies before surrender";
  Or as some tell it, *"M***e!"*

On attacks on the elite. The wording of General Cambronne's defiance in the aftermath of Waterloo is variously reported.

164.

Unpublished

With unfeigned anger he complains
  He's so misunderstood:
How can they doubt his private gains
  Are for the public good?

165.

Unpublished

In public life, there's nothing, Joyce,
So key as public trust;
So please don't make them make the choice
Of trusting you or bust.

166.

9 June 2023

You're more than happy to debase
The law into a tool;
You've made good conscience, Bob, the face
Of arbitrary rule.

167.

16 June 2022

When brave policemen stand aside
To watch them smash and rob,
When law's selectively applied,
The law has joined the mob.

168.

Unpublished

It's hard to say how deeply, Lou,
How gravely I'm appalled,
It's hard to say, 'cause if I do
You'll have my a** keel-hauled.

169.

30 June 2023

Your puppet likes to dance and play,
Your puppet even sings:
What joy, what fun, until one day
Your puppet cuts the strings.

170.

21 June 2023

Our ills are many: which is worst
Is endlessly debated:
We'd save a lot of time if first
We'd grant that they're related.

171.

13 Oct. 2022

I wished to live in bygone days,
That Athens were my home;
The gods just laughed at my malaise:
I got the fall of Rome.

172.

Unpublished

Alas, Roberto, public trust
In liberalism dwindles
As gluttony becomes disgust
At one too many swindles.

173.

31 Mar. 2022

In turn by right and left incensed,
  Soon everyone I roast;
For every day I'm most against
  Whoever's lied the most.

In those days the terms 'left' and 'right' were still used to describe political outlooks, although by then neither possessed much in the way of positive political agenda.

174.

14 Apr. 2023

Give me an old-school politics,
  Not that online narcotic,
Its addicts slavering for their fix
  Half-civic, half-psychotic.

175.

15 Dec. 2021

The trees of faction, once so green,
  Have heard the autumn call,
And singly, steadily, unseen,
  The leaves of reason fall.

176.

3 May 2022

No justice, no, not 'til it comes
  Avenging what it must:
So lest fate string us by the thumbs
  Be generous, be just.

177.

29 Apr. 2022

The news, you fret, is full of fakes,
   And every rumour's wrong;
I'll say this for the insta-takes:
   At least they don't last long.

There was a panic (one among many) in these years about 'misinformation.'

178.

30 Mar. 2022

Count this not least among the signs
   The age has come apart:
The artists are the philistines
   And censorship's an art.

179.

25 Nov. 2023

The cant, the pose, the tears, the whine,
  Threats hardly even veiled;
You'll have your way or you'll resign:
  When has that ever failed?

(Then incidentally what bliss,
  What vindication sweet
To watch the whole world stoop to kiss
  The ground before your feet!)

Yet this time — what, the tables turned?
  The calculus reversed?
Your tears dispassionately spurned?
  Your victim got there first!

Oh, I'd have warned you to beware
  But feared you'd blow a gasket—
Fate waits for every Robespierre
  Holding the same old basket.

180.

24 May 2023

At least, my friend, in times of peace,
  The truth needs no disguise;
In war disguises never cease,
  For wars are filled with lies.

Cf. Johnson *Idler* 30: 'Among the calamities of War may be justly numbered the diminution of the love of truth.'

92.

20 Mar. 2023

You stabbed me in the back, old Kurt,
  But, Kurt, that's quite OK:
I hardly care, for such a hurt
  Is easy to repay.

93.

3 July 2023

You're heading for the dance floor, Drew,
  I'll only ask you this:
You know that thing, that thing you do,
  Just give that thing a miss.

94.

3 Feb. 2023

Here let the pundit's flesh abide,
  Entombed with rites most solemn,
Immune to age, well mummifed,
  And not unlike his column.

On the long tenure of newspaper columnists.

95.

19 Apr. 2022

I feel unwell, so kindly you
  Come see me face to face,
Bringing a hundred students to
  Help diagnose my case;

A hundred icy hands they lay
  Upon my troubled brow:
I had no fever yesterday;
  I sure as hell do now.

Adapted from Martial 5.9, which seemed appropriate to the ongoing Covid epidemic: *Languebam: sed tu comitatus protinus ad me / venisti centum, Symmache, discipulis. / Centum me tetigere manus aquilone gelatae: / non habui febrem, Symmache, nunc habeo.*

181.

2 Dec. 2023

So here's one practical effect
  Your censorship's achieved:
Now even when you're quite correct
  You're never quite believed.

182.

4 Nov. 2021

"Just wealth and peace, we need no more";
  Oh, children disagree:
They claim that even civil war
  Is better than *ennui.*

183.

8 Feb. 2022

On leaders' abnegation of responsibility.

A choir is singing in the stays,
  The wheel is triple-lashed,
Along the rocks the cold wave plays,
  On them we'll soon be dashed:

For here against a cruel lee shore
  The Ship of State is pinned:
The course was safe, or so you swore;
  But now you blame the wind?

184.

1 Dec. 2022

You roll your eyes at all the fuss,
  You say we're doing great,
Reminding me 'twas ever thus—
  That smugness wrecks the state.

185.

13 Dec. 2022

"'Twas ever thus": you love that phrase,
You found it in a book;
How often, in how many ways,
It gets you off the hook!

186.

5 Jan. 2023

I fear the Goths, but you dismiss
The notion they're a threat.
Rome's safe, you say, the proof is this:
They haven't sacked it yet.

187.

21 Apr. 2023

It seems apocalypse includes
A series of delays,
And while we're striking attitudes
The universe decays.

188.

10 Feb. 2022

There's no obsession quite so strange
Nor more with sorrow fraught
Than labouring lifelong to change
The land that change forgot.

189.

4 Jan. 2023

We're satisfied with lies because
  The real no longer matters—
'Til someday soon it really does
  And then the whole thing shatters.

190.

1 Apr. 2022

Alas, do you, fair youth, still trust
  The goddess of Opinion?
I've seen the troth she pledges rust,
  For rust is her dominion.

The reference is to myths like that of Eos and Tithonus in which a goddess ensnares a youthful mortal.

191.

9 Mar. 2022

Obsessed with schemes of saving face
  And dulling His disgust,
We tremble for the human race
  To learn that God is just.

192.

29 June 2023

Far poorer centuries than mine
  Built everything to last;
Meanwhile the future shows no sign
  My century ever passed.

193.

6 Jan. 2023

Why do I feel so little rage?
  Why am I seldom vexed?
I'm skipping past the present age
  And waiting in the next.

194.

14 Apr. 2022

Bob, no fanatic ever swore
  To die behind a grouch;
There never was civil war
  Conducted from the couch;

So when they say these online trends
  Will set the land aflame,
I laugh: we know this nonsense ends
  In more of just the same.

195.

27 July 2021

He wound it up with many a frown,
  This world of human trial;
I fear that as God winds it down
  He cannot help but smile.

196.

28 Oct. 2023

No spring without a winter, Mel,
  No dawn without the night;
The gods have made us walk through hell
  Before we find delight.

From nausea at all this blood
  Our appetites increase
For what lies far beyond the mud,
  The grassy slopes of peace;

There the whole world shall rest among
  A century of flowers,
Antiquity itself made young,
  When peace at last is ours.

Our grandchildren will never know
  The numbness and the fears,
For we ourselves shall let those go
  To vanish with the years.

197.

13 Dec. 2021

Look up and breathe, be glad to see
 How time has blown away
Upon the wind of history
 The cant of yesterday.

198.

2 Mar. 2022

Stranger, to Lacedaemon make
 A journey: tell how we
Are lying here because we take
 Their standards seriously.

A translation of the epitaph for the 300 Spartans who died at Thermopylae (480 BC), attributed to Simonides: Ὦ ξεῖν', ἀγγέλλειν Λακεδαιμονίοις ὅτι τῇδε / κείμεθα, τοῖς κείνων ῥήμασι πειθόμενοι.

BOOK III

Epigrams of Ordinary Life

199.

14 Nov. 2022

Some search for meaning in their God,
  Some search for it in beauty;
But though the age may call it odd
  I found it in my duty.

200.

25 May 2023

They say our time upon this earth
  Has limits; true, but tears
And joy and rage and wit and mirth
  Make months go by like years.

201.

15 May 2023

For Mother's Day 2023.

Why parenthood? It's given me
  This infinite reward:
To drop the burden of *ennui*
  And nevermore be bored.

202.

12 Aug. 2023

So full of courage, full of fear,
   Sensing your swelling power,
You barely note the passing year:
   Youth runs from hour to hour.

My arm is weakening and my sinews
   Only half-heed my call,
And as your glorious Spring continues
   I sense the touch of Fall.

What little wisdom I've accrued
   I'll give to supplement
The passion of a passing mood,
   A joy, a discontent,

If in exchange you share that zeal
   That lifts the life of man,
Pointing it to some new ideal
   For which there is no plan:

What that may be, who you will be,
   What history it may start,
Its setbacks and its victory,
   I'll only see in part;

Yet I won't linger in the past
   When I am dead and gone;
In you, my son, my life will last
   Until you pass it on.

203.

9 June 2022

My son, you're suddenly eleven,
  No longer overawed:
What a relief, a taste of heaven,
  To learn the world is flawed!

For my son's birthday, 3 May 2022.

204.

12 Apr. 2022

So this is middle age! In youth
  My patience knew no end;
Bored now by everything but truth,
  I cannot help transcend.

205.

17 Aug. 2022

No one remembers what he reads
  For money or a grade;
Who but a costume-seller needs
  A costume post-parade?

But what is read from love or fear,
  With private joy or pain,
Will never leave the inner ear:
  Its echoes never wane.

206.

5 May 2023

With what raw zeal he teaches Greek,
  His passion just won't rest:
He knows it's that or spend a week
  Correcting every test.

On teaching Ancient Greek.

207.

15 June 2022

How many nights we've all devoted
  To wishing on a star,
While daily duties, hardly noted,
  Have made us who we are!

208.

17 Apr. 2023

I don't know in what century
  My iPhone was conceived:
If I said deep antiquity
  I know I'd be believed.

What's that? No, it's not derelict,
  It's prehistoric, mythic:
Medieval phones get merely bricked,
  Mine's gone full megalithic.

209.

28 Apr. 2023

I hoped to meet a worthy foe
  But left it far too late:
That's just the way that these things go,
  You miss 'em if you wait.

210.

17 May 2023

Infinite online content, Brett,
  And each film so well wrought;
The content's infinite and yet
  My patience, Brett, is not.

211.

9 Dec. 2022

For hours he labours to emit
The perfect tweet, imbued
With three stark facts, a touch of wit,
And just a hint of feud.

212.

4 Apr. 2023

He begged me to play hard, and I
Tragically answered Yes;
Now here I stand, well beaten by
A nine-year-old in chess.

On being beaten in chess by my son Silvan earlier that winter.

213.

24 Jan. 2023

O cruel porch pirate! Down the street,
My books in hand, you raced;
Too bad I missed the chance to meet
A thief with perfect taste.

A thief made off with my three-volume hardcover edition of Shelby Foote's *Civil War: A Narrative* when it was left at my front door by the delivery-man.

214.

15 Mar. 2023

A purr, a pounce, a minuet
Performed upon my face:
Dear Lord, what does it take to get
Some breakfast 'round this place?

On Katie, our cat.

215.

23 May 2023

You ask, Bill, how to make your rhyme
  Sound mellow, unrehearsed?
A single rule saves tons of time:
  Don't write the first line first.

216.

12 Oct. 2022

On Katie, our cat.

She likes a scratch, a long tongue-bath,
  Then sunny retroflection;
When evening falls mice feel her wrath
  And we her soft affection.

Our brains, it's true, are pretty flawed,
  Our schedules so unsteady;
We often need an extra prod
  To get her breakfast ready.

217.

6 June 2023

Task A is dull, Task B is late,
  Tasks C through K look fun;
Only when I procrastinate
  Can I get much stuff done.

218.

5 Apr. 2023

She's planted on my tousled hair
  The engine of her purr,
Prepared to leap toward the stair
  The second that I stir.

Affection's never more sincere
  Nor loyalty more real
Than when they work to commandeer
  My head before a meal.

On Katie, our cat.

219.

12 June 2023

You'll have to lash me to the mast
  As tightly as before:
Don't touch that wax until we've passed
  The Sirens' used book store;

Inside, they sing, a precious treasure
  Waits longingly for me;
Row on, my comrades, there's no leisure:
  Steer for the open sea.

220.

26 June 2023

You've put it on Kijiji, Mel,
  You've priced it through the roof;
It's far too valuable to sell:
  The listing price is proof.

Kijiji was an online marketplace, popular in Canada, in which users bought and sold items privately, featuring many bargains and some unrealistically priced items.

221.

20 Sept. 2021

The flesh is willing, but the soul
Considers with dismay
The sacred way toward the poll
Upon election day.

A federal election was held on this date.

222.

12 Jan. 2022

I steeled myself to face head-on
The variant long foretold;
But it's far worse than Omicron:
Pity a man's man-cold!

I contracted Covid at the end of 2021 but found it milder than the cold I picked up two weeks after recovering.

223.

12 May 2023

You dare me, Luba, to explain
Just why you're always right?
The truest answer sounds inane:
You're such a pleasing sight.

For my wife on her birthday, 12 May 2023.

224.

14 Sept. 2021

My sacred right, my civic voice;
But where do I begin?
How can a voter know which choice
Will help the Blue Jays win?

A federal election was held on 20 September 2021.

225.

4 July 2023 Here lies a epigrammatist,
His pessimism cured:
He boasted that he'd not be missed,
He'd find that we demurred.

226.

30 March 2024 Here is the bread, the bitter wine, Easter 2024.
The final lesson taught:
By mortal men a life divine
Is never cheaply bought.

Here is the the kiss, the traitor's kiss
Far sharper than a knife;
The kiss of death that brings new bliss,
And so the kiss of life.

Here is the hill on which slaves die,
The rebel's just reward,
The cross at which three women sigh
In mourning for their Lord.

Here is the tomb, and here the stone
That sealed the final prison,
From which You first, Lord, rose alone;
And with You we have risen

To marvel at Your greatest work,
Forever fresh and young,
The sap of spring, as petals lurk
Where once bare branches hung.

227.

23 Sept. 2022

I came for peace, I came for prayer,
  The bishop sold me merch;
Forgive me if I just won't wear
  A church's merch to church.

For Stephen Coombs.

228.

24 Jan. 2022

The pitching tunnel's full all day,
  The batting cages ring,
The astroturf is worn away
  With longing for the Spring.

Off-season indoor training.

229.

20 Dec. 2022

Day after day he gives it all,
  He sweats without complaining:
The joy of victory is small
  Beside the joy of training.

Off-season indoor training.

230.

Unpublished; Christmas 2022.

There's many gyms beneath the sun,
  But, bro, you'll travel far
Before you find reps half as fun
  As reps at OLR.

Our family's baseball gym has for many years been *One Last Rep* (OLR) in Dartmouth, Nova Scotia.

231.

14 Feb. 2022

If you're insatiable demand,
Then I'm untold supply:
It's thanks, my love, to th' Unseen Hand
That what I sell you buy.

Economist's Love Song, for Valentine's Day.

232.

19 Apr. 2023

The baseball gods for months have blessed
St. Dominic's bright isle,
And even in the cool Midwest
They've played for quite a while;

Here, as the petals first poke free,
The fields are almost dry:
Here we still slam balls off the tee,
Tick off the days, and sigh.

St. Dominic's isle is Hispaniola, location of the Dominican Republic, which takes its name from its capital city, Santo Domingo.

233.

25 Mar. 2023

No, Spring, there is no going back:
I'm ready now to sigh
To hear a hanging curveball crack
Across the freshest sky.

First hint of baseball weather.

234.

17 June 2022

It landed deep, he didn't slow,
To first— then second— more—
I saw them drop the cut-off throw
And knew my son would score.

11U teams do not always hit the cut-off man, resulting in more frequent inside-the-park home runs.

235.

8 Apr. 2022

The day has come: open the Dome,
  I'll get the dogs and beers:
'Cause Vladdy's bat is coming home
  To forty thousand cheers.

Poor Texas Rangers, you assumed
  You'd face our old bullpen?
Alas, alas, your lineup's doomed —
  Except for Semien.

You think your pitching will suffice
  When Bo and Teo call?
George, Lourdes, Vlad? Take my advice
  And simply walk them all.

The Blue Jays' home opener, 2022. Bo is Bo Bichette, power-hitting shortstop; Teo is Teo Hernandez, Lourdes is Lourdes Gurriel Jr., and George is George Springer, all outfielders; Vlad is Vladimir Guerrero Jr., slugging first-baseman. Semien is Marcus Semien, a great second basemen we had lost to Texas in the off-season. The Jays did not do as well that year as hoped.

236.

11 Apr. 2023

The Dome's rebuilt, the weather's fine,
  The Jays are home to win:
Let every superstar align,
  Let history begin.

The Blue Jays' home opener, 2023. Their stadium, informally known as the SkyDome, had been renovated in the off-season. Expectations for the team were high, but the Jays did not do as well that year as hoped.

237.

23 March 2024

Like Troy, the AL East is stacked:
  The Sox, the fearsome Rays,
The Orioles have made their pact
  To stop the mighty Jays:

Aye, oaths unbreakable they've sworn,
  Summoning none too soon
The pinstriped legion, smooth and shorn,
  The tricky sons of Boone:

See, there's tall Judge, and at his side
  The shuffling Soto swings,
There's great Arozarena's pride,
  And Rutschman's clear voice rings:

At least 'til Vladdy draws his bat,
  Dread of the Caribbean,
And he whom Dante B. begat,
  Our flowing-haired Achaean;

Let the division flee before
  Our glorious pitching staff:
The baseball gods know what's in store:
  They love us and they laugh.

The AL East certainly was stacked once again in 2024, but the Jays did not do as well that year as hoped. The "pinstriped legion" are the Yankees, managed by Aaron Boone; "he whom Dante B. begat, / Our flowing-haired Achaean" is Bo Bichette.

238.

11 Mar. 2022

The war, the shortages, inflation:
  So much is out of whack;
And yet my soul finds recreation
  Now that the baseball's back.

Baseball had been greatly interrupted by the Covid epidemic of 2020–2021.

239.

22 Apr. 2022

On over-eagerness at the plate.

You wonder if your bat's to blame,
  Or maybe it's your swing?
The fact is, Bob, it's all the same:
  You swing at everything.

240.

4 May 2024

For my older son on his 13th birthday.

So it's official: he's thirteen,
  And thirteen with aplomb:
His shoulders broad, his brow serene,
  He's taller than his mom,

As distant now from World War I
  As I was from Riel;
For him the battle's just begun,
  For me it ain't gone well:

Like me, I hope, he'll strive to fix
  Faults of the human heart,
And then, like me, find politics
  Is nothing without art:

In art our failure is redeemed
  As tragedy, the proof
The gods are realer than we dreamed
  And never stand aloof.

241.

1 Sept. 2022

You want to hit more dingers, Mark?
Just use your common sense:
When everything's inside the park,
It's time to move the fence.

Written together with my younger son, Silvan.

242.

12 July 2022

I crossed a mighty bridge, my friend,
Drove up into the sky:
Heaven was on the other end
And it was PEI.

On crossing the Confederation Bridge onto Prince Edward Island from New Brunswick. While ascending to the level of the main bridge, the driver has the impression of driving up into the sky.

243.

29 Aug. 2022

Before I pitched, to conquer doubt,
I asked a priest of Zen
Just how I ought to strike them out:
He said, "Not how but when."

I.e. "now." I had bought a parcel of used books on Zen and found them very useful for baseball. In pitching, I adopted the last four words here as my mantra.

244.

Unpublished

A man of bronze, a man of myth,
As tough as tough can get,
So long as I'm provided with
Enough Robaxacet.

On playing ball in middle age.

245.

25 May 2024

On being two-hit by the White Sox on 21 May 2024, a team that would go on set the all-time record for most games lost in a season by an MLB team.

A sin to triumph? Some might say
  Our Monday triumph earned
That grim shellacking yesterday,
  Our hubris overturned.

The strike-out king shall be struck out,
  The picker off picked off,
The champion of yore shall pout,
  The also-ran shall scoff.

Perhaps a higher justice rules
  The leagues of earth we plod;
Perhaps the eagerness of fools
  Amuses every god;

Perhaps the Jays' front office needs
  A tragic policy,
Replacing analytic creeds
  With cold theology.

246.

7 Sept. 2022

Authority of the umps.

Accept it or protest, my friend,
  Fight back or take your lumps,
On every diamond, in the end,
  The Lord is with the umps.

247.

5 Sept. 2022

On fan psychology.

Coincidence you call it, Lee,
  Yet by one fact I'm struck:
Our wins are always destiny,
  Our losses always luck.

248.

18 May 2024

A Rockwellesque scenario, not based on a particular grandma. Dartmouth is the perennial rival of Halifax baseball teams.

After the struggle of a game,
  I notice Grandma's grin—
Although she loves us just the same—
  Is wider when we win.

Her voice is always warm, of course,
  So after Caius' double,
Her voice that evening was so hoarse
  I thought we were in trouble.

Then later, in the championship,
  I got the walk-off hit:
The parents watched her old hands rip
  What she'd sat down to knit.

But best is when, when things go wrong
  Against all likelihood
And Dartmouth wins, her hug's so long
  It proves that we're still good.

249.

16 Sept. 2022

The hitter sits without a sound
  As fans high five and shout:
For every K-strut off the mound
  Some poor guy just struck out.

On the zero-sum of the pitcher-hitter confrontation.

250.

19 June 2023

Fear not, my son: the Jays are strong,
  And though we're near the bottom,
The spring is ending, summer's long:
  What matters is the autumn.

It turns out my son was correct in fearing for the Jays' chances.

251.

4 Nov. 2022

The leg, the hip, the hand, the eye
  Help put it past the wall,
But only one thing makes it fly:
  The will to smash the ball.

On hitting the ball hard.

252.

15 June 2023

The pitcher aimed me at the plate,
  Around me cool air rushed;
The crack, the cheers: turns out my fate
  Was simply to be crushed.

Inscription for a home run ball.

253.

29 May 2023

No, God Himself can't bring it back,
  Can't make it halt or fall:
Not matter how you curse it, Zach,
  That there's a home run ball.

For Zach Wells, a keen fellow player.

254.

28 June 2023

We sometimes pitch, we sometimes hit,
  You never know just which;
By God those guys are in for it
  The day we hit *and* pitch.

255.

17 Feb. 2023

Devoted, free of qualm or quirk,
  Mystical in his aim,
In perfect union with his work,
  He throws a perfect game.

The perfect game.

256.

13 July 2024

On playing baseball in Nova Scotian weather.

Aye, let the whole Atlantic cloud
  Pour down upon the field,
Umbrellas sprout among the crowd:
  Shall Nova Scotians yield?

Not with the count at three and two,
  And not with Bond at bat,
And then McPherson's next, who's due,
  And Mitchell after that.

Play on! the sodden umpire calls,
  As jerseys stick to skins:
When water's flying off the balls
  The real baseball begins.

In semi-hurricanes we play,
  Through mud our wet cleats slog;
Could well be worse, the players all say:
  At least it's not the fog.

257.

7 Oct. 2023

On losing to the Twins in the 2023 wildcard game.

Our God hath spread no easy path
  For pilgrims of the Jays:
Up heights of bliss, down depths of wrath
  We pick our lonely ways:

One day our guys go four for five,
  The next our bats go quiet;
One day we roast our foes alive,
  The next they just run riot.

We do not ask for much, dear Lord,
  Still less a hundred wins;
But how is it the offence scored
  Just once against the Twins?

The dread of sin will stir the folk
  To penitential lashes;
But I'll put on my sackcloth cloak
  And wallow in the ashes.

258.

10 Oct. 2022

In a wildcard series against the Mariners, the Jays lost a nightmarish last game, blowing an 8–1 lead (8 October 2022).

What can you say? The Baseball Gods
  Care nothing for our griefs;
The same Olympic mob applauds
  Each bolt that burns the Leafs.

259.

14 Feb. 2022

Around him hung a stillness that
  She'd heard somewhere before,
Between the cracking of the bat
  And then the home-run roar.

A Valentine's Day baseball poem.

260.

28 Oct. 2022

At last the pitcher's fastball wearies,
  The bats swing cold and slow;
Time to go watch the World Series
  Before it starts to snow.

Fall Ball in Canada.

261.

26 Oct. 2024

Now let the storm and lightning flash,
  Now let November come;
For when the mighty Titans clash,
  One Titan must succumb:

Now Mookie, Freddie, Smith, and Lux
  Keep up the fabled story,
With Shohei of the billion bucks
  Who aims for only glory;

Yet Judge awaits, and Jazz, and Soto,
  And Stanton's giant frame;
They do not fear quick Yamamoto,
  Nor Flaherty's bright fame.

Yet as fans cheer, another crowd
  Politely sits and waits,
So quiet in a place so loud:
  The silent row of greats,

There Joe and Yogi watch in peace,
  With Whitey, Mickey too,
And Snider, Campanella, Reese,
  And #42.

Let's watch beside such men: let fools
  On politics go numb.
We'll celebrate a game with rules
  And let November come.

Anticipating the 2024 World Series (on the eve of the US presidential election) between the Yankees and the Dodgers, which was certainly epic, although more lopsided than this poem had foreseen. The second and third stanzas name Dodgers and Yankee stars respectively; Joe (DiMaggio), Yogi (Berra), Whitey (Ford), and Mickey (Mantle) are Yankee greats of yore, while (Duke) Snider, (Roy) Campanella, (Pee Wee) Reese, and (Jackie Robinson) #42 are Dodgers greats.

262.

7 June 2022

We win, we lose; we lose, we win;
  All glory tends to par;
A season ends, but we begin
  A new trip 'round a star.

On the near-inevitability of failure in sports.

263.

16 Sept. 2023

Hair cut, bags stuffed with fresh supplies,
  Their sneakers scrubbed or new,
Too serious to satirize,
  Too giddy to be blue,

They gather from the summer street
  To find the old school yard
Considerably smaller, meet
  The new guys and regard

The girls who huddle by the door
  Rapt in a hurricane
Of conversation; something more
  Is there, but who'll explain?

At last the bell, the worn-down stairs,
  The flag, the board, the glue,
The seats that this year shall be theirs —
  The comfort of the new.

Grade 5, Day 1.

264.

31 Aug. 2024

The Summer came, the Summer's done:
  Into the Fall we leap;
For at the end of summer fun
  Not many parents weep.

New haircut, shoes, a whole new year
  He can't wait to begin:
It brings a sentimental tear
  And somewhat giddy grin.

But soon the quiet house is clean,
  The laundry's put away,
The car is polished to a sheen,
  There's time for the café;

And then by silence satiated
  We ask where Summer went,
Wishing to God it never faded,
  Missing the days well spent.

265.

28 Sept. 2021

And so she's launched: it's bittersweet
  To watch my new-wrought poem
Sail off to join the storm-wracked fleet
  Of Ancient Greece and Rome.

My epic poem, *The Odyssey of Star Wars*, a blank-verse retelling of the Skywalker saga in 8000 lines, was published on 28 September 2021.

266.

19 Sept. 2022

On the cusp of Autumn.

Now soon the vivid symphony
Of autumn will begin;
The tuning of a crimson tree
Its first soft violin.

267.

12 Oct. 2024

Thanksgiving 2024.

For each and every little blessing,
The nation now gives thanks
As much as for this first-rate dressing:
The peace, the solvent banks,

The loyal colonels, humble spies,
Long-winded editorials,
Intolerance of public lies,
Our well kept war memorials,

A prairie summer day's last light,
The peaks from English Bay,
The arctic wilderness of white,
The Cabot Trail's tall spray,

For these give thanks: pull up a chair:
Although we disagree,
Tonight a hearty feast we'll share
With friends from sea to sea.

268.

3 Nov. 2022

The trunk is numb, the branches bare,
The flame of autumn gone,
Yet every twig is well aware
A spring will someday dawn.

269.

17 Dec. 2021

Picking out a Christmas tree.

It's plenty tall enough, says she,
To give that Christmas feeling—
As if it's Christmas with a tree
That doesn't scrape the ceiling!

270.

23 Dec. 2022

The inn at Bethlehem.

The beds are comfy, get some sleep.
Thank God they still had space!
Always a catch, though: sounds like sheep
Are loose behind the place.

The light, the singers? Let them be,
No point in scolding them;
We'll get some sleep, sleep in, then see
The sights of Bethlehem.

271.

23 Dec. 2023

Christmas Day 2023. The poem closely follows Luke 2:1–19.

And in those days it came to pass
  That Caesar did decree
A tax on every clan and class,
  And so from Galilee

Young Joseph journeyed, to the place
  Of David, Bethlehem,
For Joseph was of David's race,
  A leaf on Jesse's stem.

And with him Mary came, his wife,
  Across the leagues of earth;
And in her was another life,
  And she would give it birth;

And yet the inn was full that day,
  She swathed him and she set
That infant on a bed of hay;
  And there before him met

The shepherds, full of joy and fright:
  They tell of angels singing
That Christ the Lord was born that night
  And all the stars were ringing;

But Mary, Mary young and wise,
  When shepherds all depart,
She looks into her baby's eyes
  And ponders in her heart.

272.

23 Dec. 2021

The shepherds.

This infant was not born to bless
  A palace or a crown,
For He was sent in helplessness
  To some suburban town;

Poor shepherds only can afford
  To hear the heavens sing
That now there is a different lord,
  There is a different king.

273.

27 Dec. 2021

Santa's visit.

The milk is gone, the cookies chewed,
  But each year he becomes
More shocked that Santa'd be so rude
  To leave so many crumbs.

274.

26 Dec. 2022

The Three Wise Men.

Too long, I think, we've sat enthralled
  By study of the sky:
Saddle the beasts, my friends: we're called:
  Let's go discover why.

275.

24 Dec. 2021 — The Three Wise Men.

However grim the online trends,
  However bleak the news
To which the arc of history bends,
  The moral arc pursues

A distant justice: note the star,
  Follow it as you roam
Toward a place where angels are,
  Toward another home:

No palace and no temple but
  A dirty, broken shed,
A manger and a light and what
  Will banish death and dread;

Then be a better worshipper
  Than who you came to be,
Offering no francincense, no myrrh,
  Only humility.

276.

2 Jan. 2023 — New Year's 2022.

My resolutions? First, to pick
  Some good ones, good and strong;
Second, to get them over quick:
  The best ones don't last long.

277.

6 Jan. 2024

New Year's 2023.

Is this the year my plans are spoiled,
  The year my hopes are dashed?
Shall every patient scheme be foiled,
  Each resolution trashed?

Probably: what's more normal than
  Hopes ending in a sigh?
A resolution, like a man,
  Is only born to die.

Yet, even as they laugh, the gods
  Prepare to shed a tear,
Watching as we defy the odds
  In claiming our new year:

Bring on the lentils and the weights,
  The online politesse:
No matter what grim fate awaits
  I'll take short-term success.

278.

10 Aug. 2024

On getting your own room and the transition to teenagehood.

The time has come: he's now a teen,
  Wiser than we assume;
The time has come, so long foreseen:
  He's getting his own room.

Some books he's leaving with his brother,
  The trophy nook divided
With many a smile for one another,
  All easily decided.

Yet then we reach that special shelf
  Where long ago he set
The trophies that he made himself
  Through days of toil and sweat,

The Lego ships, dusty but proud,
  Some tiny, some immense,
Which childhood fancy once endowed
  With deep significance:

Now nevermore to sail the waves,
  They all must tumble in,
Except the red ship: something saves
  The red ship from the bin.

279.

17 May 2022

So how come everybody blames
  Old age? It sounds just great:
At last I can forget the names
  Of half the guys I hate.

280.

24 May 2021

There's many things I'll never do:
  To read in Japanese,
To go to war, to wield a cue,
  To look like Hercules,

To write an anthem, guide a state,
  Or cut a tyrant's throat,
In outer space to levitate,
  To steer a giant boat.

Let others wander, others roam,
  Thank God that I committed
To wife and children and a home:
  I saw my duty; did it.

BOOK IV

Poems for Particular Occasions

281.

6 Apr. 2024

On the third annivesary of *The Hub,* which coincided with a solar eclipse.

The sun is gobbled from the sky,
  The frightened priests presage
With many a malcontented sigh
  The ending of an age

Of journalism: soon they'll print
  No news, no sports, no arts,
The paper shrinks, the owner's skint,
  The readership departs;

And all the vows of Ottawa,
  The pleas of desperate lips
Are made in vain: a harsher law
  Lies back of this eclipse.

But look! Now Sean and Rudyard climb
  The pyramid's vast stair,
And at the peak, with rite sublime,
  They chant their mighty prayer:

The sun, thanks to *The Hub*'s clear spell,
  Returns to bless the earth;
After three years, who won't foretell
  The fourth estate's rebirth?

282.

4 Nov. 2023

On Stuart Thomson's moving on from being editor of *The Hub* (the frigate) to a new job at the *National Post* (the 74).

The captain's got a new command,
  We pipes him down the side;
There's not an officer nor hand
  As watches that dry-eyed;

Aye, she's a fine old man-of-war—
  Ship of the line, that's right;
Why, bless you, yes, a 74,
  A ship that likes to fight;

But look, he turns, and there's his hat,
  Salutes us from the boat;
He knows there's not a frigate that
  Can beat us, none afloat;

And that's his doing, lad: this crew
  He trained — oh, we was green! —
To make all sail, to point 'em true,
  And sweep the ocean clean.

So here's my hat, dear captain, too,
  And here's another cheer:
It's been all joy to sail with you;
  And here's another tear!

283.

7 Jan. 2022

Someday as we perhaps review
  Bright history's fading page
We'll marvel we ourselves once knew
  Th' Elizabethan Age,

When she who was at first a girl
  Enthroned in royal beauty
Through seven decades' storm and swirl
  Taught the frail world its duty;

And whosoever, centuries hence,
  With every step and breath
Upholds the crown's magnificence
  Shall be Elizabeth.

6 February 2022 was the 70th anniversary of Queen Elizabeth's coronation. This poem, besides being published in *The Hub*, was sent to her as a tribute.

284.

9 Sept. 2022

Farewell, Elizabeth. One throne
  Endures forever: go
And greet the monarch who alone
  Can all your virtue know.

As Alfred's sword once taught his land
  Never to bow or yield,
So simple patience, in your hand,
  Became your people's shield.

With patience now we must endure
  A sadness long foreseen,
Relieved at least to be so sure
  God's saved you, dearest Queen.

Queen Elizabeth II died on 8 September 2022.

285.

20 Sept. 2022

She's buried, Luba: dry your tears:
  At Windsor let her sleep
Beside her father; neither hears
  This world of mortals weep.

The Queen's funeral took place on 19 September 2022.

286.

8 May 2023

Upon his lips a binding vow,
  Beneath his throne a stone,
A mighty crown upon his brow,
  Its burden his alone;

And we, until the world may cease
  Or blend the earth and sea,
Will wear like diadems of peace
  Our oaths of loyalty.

God save the King, the priest has said;
  The ancient walls resound;
And as he stands, the people's head
  By Charles the Third is crowned.

The coronation of Charles III took place on 6 May 2023.

287.

10 Feb. 2024

On the King's illness.

You've blamed the folly of the age
  With reason, not with wrath;
Part king, part architect, part sage,
  You've shown a different path;

Yet this, if this alone, may claim
  History's eternal prize:
Today our surgeons heal the lame,
  The sickly sleep and rise

Refreshed as from a passing dream;
  No more the diabetic
Staggers, no more poor patients scream
  For want of anaesthetic;

No more this nation need despair
  To learn that you are ill,
Entrusting to wise doctors' care
  Our dear king, come what will.

288.

29 Sept. 2021

On the human propensity to war.

It seems they only go to war
  Because they can forget
The peace they swore for evermore:
  Remember or regret.

289.

23 Aug. 2021

On the withdrawal of Western forces from Afghanistan after a war of nearly 20 years against the Taliban, a faction of extreme cultural and religious conservatives.

So Maryam will be veiled again
And Ghulam crucified
Because he trusted in the pen
A generous West supplied;

Again the population thrills
To see God's hand is hard;
'Til some new factions win the hills,
Its cities to bombard.

Think not, triumphant Taliban,
That your success was fated:
Toward the overreach of Man
God's vengeance is not sated:

Though slow, in its totality
It comes, it comes: 'tis sweet
To revel in your victory,
But think of our defeat.

290.

14 Oct. 2023

On the outbreak of the Israel-Hamas war of 2023. A hymn to Ares.

In every shadow, Lord, you wait,
  Dark as an ancient stain,
A place unlit, except by hate,
  The shadows of the brain;

You sound like rifles being cocked,
  Hands raised to no avail,
The spattering blood, the victim mocked,
  The orphan's long, low wail.

You are the killer and the killed,
  The bullet and the gore,
The laughter at beloved blood spilled:
  You are the Lord of War.

Far from the temples of the rest,
  Far from the city's heart
Your sanctuary sits, Lord, lest
  You tear the whole apart.

291.

5 Oct. 2024

On the Israel-Hamas war.

Murderers think that war is best,
But soon they learn to grieve:
For War is an obnoxious guest
Who overstays his leave.

This is a party of the dead,
Those gone, those yet to go;
To Death himself the bride is wed,
And he reaps what we sow.

And Conquest follows after him,
And Famine in the rear;
Their horses make the day grow dim,
The heavens disappear,

And then the poor sea creatures drown,
Earth blazes, mountains quake,
Fire from the riven sky rains down,
Just as the prophet spake.

'Tis but a vision of the soul;
Are visions never real?
If it disgusts you, keep the scroll
And do not break the seal.

292.

28 Feb. 2022

Sleep well, my son, oh, sleep so tight,
  Far from the thump of guns,
Far from the ruin that tonight
  Claims other people's sons.

The Russo-Ukrainian war began on 24 February 2022.

293.

28 Feb. 2022

Kiev must fall to bombs and brawn,
  You'd like us to believe;
But that Kiev is long-since gone:
  You're now besieging Kyiv.

'Kiev' is the Russian name of the city, 'Kyiv' the Ukrainian; in the first month of the war, its Ukrainian defenders threw back Russian tank columns from the west and north-east.

294.

23 Feb. 2022

He marched in half a million men,
  His empire to secure;
Ten thousand marched back out again,
  Still shouting, *Vive l'Empereur!*

On the folly of sending large armies across the steppe, whether in 1812 or in 2022.

295.

13 Apr. 2022

I fear that fans of drama yearn
  To see their heroes dead;
But shouldn't heroism earn
  The right to die in bed?

On the somewhat ghoulish enthusiasm for the war in non-combatant nations.

296.

16 Mar. 2022

Make peace before your armour sinks
  Into the April mud,
Before the Muse of History blinks
  And sees you're just a dud.

After the initial Russian columns were repulsed in the West, it looked like Putin had an opportunity to make peace; instead he embarked on a war of attrition in the Donbas region of eastern Ukraine.

297.

28 Sept. 2022

You say you've got a million men,
  And, Vlad, I'm sure you're right;
I'm just not sure it matters when
  Those men don't want to fight.

On the poor morale of the Russian conscripts.

298.

2 Mar. 2023

Well, China's seldom launched a war,
  And I won't say it would;
Yet it could never win before,
  And now, I fear, it could.

In 2023, concern arose that China would seize the opportunity of the Russo-Ukrainian war to invade Taiwan.

299.

27 Jan. 2024

The pixels will absorb his days:
  Such is the console's claim;
So distant from the ancient ways,
  This young man no aim;

But does she miss him? No, she's got
  Her Insta and her cake,
The other future left to rot
  For present comfort's sake:

A pair that never meets or mates,
  No husband and no wife,
For so the Internet negates
  The former love of life.

Not caviar, not crisp Champagne
  But endless satiation,
That's luxury today, the bane
  Of every richer nation;

And this shall be our legacy,
  The mark of our collapse:
"Here lies the postwar century:
  It dearly loved its apps."

300.

22 July 2022

Ah, climate change! Of course it's rude
  What Carlin once opined:
Though we ourselves may well be screwed,
  The Earth will hardly mind.

Adapted from George Carlin: *There is nothing wrong with the planet, nothing wrong with the planet. The planet is fine; the people are f--ked! Difference!*

301.

4 July 2022

Someday the Earth will be relieved
  To shed the human horde,
Her boundless beauty unperceived,
  Her privacy restored.

302.

9 Jan. 2023

So Pelé has been taken up,
  The angels sing and dance:
For next time, at the next World Cup,
  They've finally got a chance.

The legendary Brazilian soccer star Pelé died on 29 December 2022 at the age of 82.

303.

24 June 2022

Tomorrow he was born who breathed
  Love for the English rose;
To later ages he bequeathed
  The flower of his prose.

RIP George Orwell (1903–1950), born on 25 June.

304.

18 Nov. 2022

The years have raised, the years transform
  This maple proud and tall;
The years will bring a final storm
  In which it too must fall.

305.

2 June 2023

Come, angel of the rain, and soak
  The forests with your pity;
Come free us from the smokes that choke
  Your most devoted city.

In early June 2023, wildfires destroyed large tracts of forest to the immediate west of Halifax.

306.

27 July 2024

The pine-clad slopes still arch aloft,
  And there's the Pyramid;
The light of aftermath, now soft,
  Shows what the brown haze hid.

As pitiless as war sweeps down,
  Just so the great fire came
To wrap the mountains' fairest town
  In smoke, and then in flame.

Now ruins, where the houses stood,
  Poke through the morning mists,
As if this were a neighborhood
  For archaeologists,

Who'll say, "These ashes in a line?
  That's when the fire went through;
The bricks above it, that's the sign
  They made it good as new!"

Lament for Jasper.

307.

4 Apr. 2022

They asked what landing we'd prefer;
  I said, As soft as soft;
But every other passenger
  Would rather stay aloft.

On support for the ongoing housing bubble by property holders.

308.

1 Feb. 2022

Sure, wave the maple leaf thro' town
  And honk until you're blue;
But if you hang it upside down
  I'll do the same to you.

On 29 January, a large convoy of heavy trucks installed itself around Parliament Hill in Ottawa, honking noisily, in protest at ongoing Covid restrictions. Some protesters were flying the Maple Leaf upside down.

309.

2 Feb. 2022

The leaders say they will not lead
  If people won't obey;
The people say they do not need
  Weak leaders anyway.

One of the abiding mysteries of the trucker protests was the lack of response by any level of government, evidently from fear of escalation.

310.

24 Feb. 2022

It was a bold experiment
  Conceived in loyalty:
Peace, order, and good government;
  At least we're one for three.

"Peace, Order, and Good Government" is the informal motto of the Canadian constitution.

311.

6 Dec. 2022

I fear that populism, Ern,
  Is nothing but the ease
With which the people now discern
  Your phony expertise.

312.

17 Feb. 2022

You sure talk tough, but then, alas,
  You never come to act;
A leader ought to kick some a**
  But kick it with great tact.

The Prime Minister indicated he would act vigorously against the protests, now in their third week, but failed to do so; whereas such situations in fact call for vigorous action accompanied by soothing rhetoric.

313.

10 Mar. 2022

Poor Bob, I wish you would invent
  A fresher tragic flaw
Than vindicating government
  By mutilating law.

The Government invoked the *Emergencies Act* on 14 February, without (in many people's view) providing sufficient reason for doing so, as required by the Act. This began a process whereby the protesters were eventually removed peacefully.

314.

22 Nov. 2022

You judge our economic strength
By GDP, poor Nate,
As if you judged a book by length
Or human health by weight.

315.

8 Dec. 2022

Salute the genius who perceived
Most problems countrywide
Would be at least a bit relieved
By widespread suicide.

Perhaps the most abhorrent development in Canada in 2022 was the extension of the assisted suicide programme to include not merely the terminally ill but those suffering from corrigible social and economic ills.

316.

22 Feb. 2023

So, Rod, it turns out you're a spy;
Of course that's rather odd:
But surely odder still is why
Your codename should be "Rod."

In February 2023, leaks apparently from within CSIS suggested that a former minister in the government of Ontario had had ties with Chinese intelligence, which had given him the somewhat transparent codename of 'the Minister.'

317.

8 June 2023

It's true, of course, mistakes were made,
  Don't know by whom or when,
Or why, or how; so I'm afraid
  They're being made again.

This poem appeared during the scandal on Chinese interference in Canadian elections, but the evasion of responsibility depicted is perennial.

318.

31 May 2023

In ancient King Jugurtha's tale
  One dictum I admire:
That any city up for sale
  Is bound to find a buyer.

The Chinese interference scandal made it clear that much of the Canadian establishment preferred its investments in China to an assertion of Canadian independence.

319.

28 Mar. 2023

Believe me, Bob, I'm baffled too:
  How ever could it be
That anyone suspected you
  Of any loyalty?

320.

9 Sept. 2023

RIP Terry Fox (1958–1981); composed while driving from Ottawa to Halifax.

Luba, the miles of our long way
  Flash past so fleetingly:
This weary journey takes one day,
  Which took him forty-three.

The biting wind, the parching sun
  He felt, and did not tire,
Filled with the will to live, to run,
  Filled with a lofty fire:

Your Rama and your Hercules,
  Your Roland and Guan Yu,
Have long since put him at his ease
  Among the very few.

And there the road still calls him, bright
  As our road ever shone:
He's on the Marathon of Light
  And started before dawn.

321.

2 Dec. 2023

RIP Sir Isaac Brock (1769–1812).

His coat and sash, my mates, my fears,
  The heat, the powder smell;
He cried, "Push on, York Volunteers!"
  And instantly he fell;

Still up the Heights we pushed, we few,
  Into the hellish noise,
And some we scattered, some we slew:
  "Revenge the General, boys!"

Yet now some Fenian, young Ben Lett,
  Has bombed the monument,
As if without it we'd forget
  The blood that brave men spent

To keep us safe from Yankee tricks:
  The spot where Brock was killed
Endures forever, and those bricks
  Are easy to rebuild

So long as men of York perceive
  The origin of beauty,
So long as men of York believe
  That glory comes from duty.

322.

17 Feb. 2024

Ode to Sir Charles Tupper (1821–1915).

Bewhiskered Ram of Cumberland,
  Swift ship that none could scupper,
O voice of order orotund,
  O brave Sir Charles Tupper,

We still remember how your toil
  Inspired Confederation,
How against Howe you strove to foil
  New Scotland's abnegation.

You gave us schools, and many a deal,
  And sure diplomacy,
The silver ribbon of bright steel
  That reached the distant sea.

By crisis hastily installed,
  You faced young Laurier,
Too late to highest office called,
  Too quickly whisked away.

323.

1 March 2024

RIP Brian Mulroney (1939–2024).

No passive King: he was a Rook,
  Eater of petty pawns;
At his approach the whole board shook;
  His was an Age of Bronze,

Of tragic sieges, massive fleets,
  Whole cities staked on glory,
Great victories, aye, and great defeats,
  All for a deathless story;

And I was there, a little lad
  Intent on every speech,
Asking my ever patient dad
  The latest news of Meech,

Proud to be from a polity
  So eager to evolve;
That found in every mystery
  A riddle we could solve.

That was his time: he gave the will
  To build, to soar, to dig;
Mulroney's gone, but maybe still
  Like him we'll dare go big.

324.

15 Sept. 2021

Here lies old Norm. Don't worry, folks:
  That rustle in the breeze?
It's only Norm, and at his jokes
  The dead begin to wheeze.

RIP Norm MacDonald (1959–2021), the great Canadian comedian, who had died the day before.

325.

17 Aug. 2024

Unbeatable, he heard the beat
  Of Paris: like a bird
Untouched by worldly defeat
  He winged the ocean, lured

To join the athletes of the field,
  Swift swimmers, boxers bold
In chasing sleepless dreams that yield
  A podium of gold.

There like a water spout that twists
  Far out on English Bay,
On toes and knees and head and wrists
  He flowed, he whirled away

His rivals' hopes. Deathless renown
  Means little, though, to him;
I saw a higher glory crown
  The Wizard, Philip Kim.

Ode to Phil Wizard, Canadian gold medallist in Breaking at the Paris Olympic Games.

326.

15 June 2024

On Edmonton's attempted comeback in the Stanley Cup Finals.

O doorway to the northern world,
  City of liquid gold,
Those pennants o'er your rink unfurled
  To youthful ears have told

The tales of Kurri and of Fuhr,
  And Coffey, Messier,
And sleek and calm and hard and sure
  The One, who went away;

If any city, any team
  Can battle back from this
And inch by inch win back the dream,
  And fill the streets with bliss,

It's Edmonton: there is a Cup
  And that Cup has a home,
And when they'll hang the pennant up
  No more the Cup need roam.

327.

29 Jun 2024

On the Oilers' loss in Game 7.

If every season were the best,
  If every dream came true,
If every uniform were blessed,
  If every sky were blue,

That would be heaven—not sports, my friend:
  A fan is born to ache:
And always, at the season's end,
  A fan's brave heart must break,

Save when, perhaps, a golden light
  Is shed by heaven's king,
A brief shaft, bright amid the night,
  And choirs of angels sing

A championship. Yet even then
  All champions soon go slack,
And last year's vanquished rise again:
  These Oilers will be back:

At last, on some Dominion Day,
  They'll hook our nation up,
Returning it from far away,
  Our long-lost silver Cup.

328.

20 Apr. 2024

On the new budget.

I must admit it's kind of funny,
  Your plan to court the youth:
You'll try to bribe them with their money
  When all they want is truth.

You're baffled at their weird malaise,
  At how they storm and yell
That they'll soon take your sunny ways
  And drop them down a well.

Is this young people's gratitude
  For all those photo-ops?
You worry, if they get too rude,
  You'll have to call the cops:

A plan worn down by overuse,
  The old golpista shtick:
You'll spend vast sums on carrot juice
  Backed up by loads of stick.

329.

8 June 2024

On the Narcissus of Canadian politics.

He was the prince, and damsels swooned
  From coast to shining coast;
But time and fickle fortune wound
  The vanity of most;

The people cheered to see him box
  Or surf the waves so bold,
But now the people change the locks
  And leave him in the cold.

Alas, one day, the mirror smiled
  And won his noble heart,
Himself by his own self beguiled,
  And ne'er the twain shall part:

Aye, let the damsels swoon no more,
  The people's wrath be grim:
He'll take what heaven has in store
  So long as he's with him.

330.

13 Apr. 2024

On champagne socialism.

Please tell me that this guy's a spoof,
This leading socialist,
His silky thread-count through the roof,
A Rolex on his wrist:

For even as the latest phase
Of populism rages,
He's out there cooking up new ways
To stifle workers' wages:

Lest the harsh market's fresh demands
Should make his patrons pay,
He'll bring in millions of new hands
From half a world away;

Then he'll still get to play the saint,
Rich helper of the poor;
Letting the market help? That ain't
Got quite the same allure.

331.

14 Sept. 2024

Allegory of the Canadian political situation.

The emperor has lost our trust,
  His glory swiftly dwindles,
His court an object of disgust,
  That net of crimes and swindles;

And couriers too he sends out east
  The eastern troops to summon;
The couriers prove one thing at least:
  The eastern troops ain't comin'.

The Germans cross the weak frontier,
  And Spain has backed his cousin,
And Otho's landing in the rear
  With cohorts by the dozen.

The recklessness, the sins of pride,
  These things fate carved in stone,
The pleas, the tears, the suicide,
  That day he took the throne.

For heaven will suffer no man's reign
  To last forever, Nick:
But always we start fresh again:
  The clock begins to tick.

332.

9 March 2024

On the cognitive decline of Joe Biden.

A single glare beneath his brow
Once used to stop 'em cold:
But now his cape is threadbare, now
The matador is old:

His blade is dull, his eyes unclear,
His shuffle deadly slow;
Yet still th' aficionados cheer
And shout, "Go get him, Joe!"

Meanwhile the old bull's rage is fringed
With madness: watch him run,
His horns so crooked, his snorts unhinged,
Five Ferdinands in one,

Charging the gate, the solid wall,
Oblivious of his foe;
And meanwhile in the stands they call,
"Go on, go get him, Joe!"

333.

2 Nov. 2024

On the eve of the US presidential election.

Your question: Trump or Harris? Sit
  Before my tripod stool;
The god will only answer it
  With riddles: 'tis the rule.

Ever more swiftly down the stream
  We paddle past the vines;
Deeper and deeper into dream
  We tumble, seeking signs

That slip away; relentless foes
  Are gaining ground behind;
The rising generation knows
  No peace, no peace of mind.

An angel's coming to collect
  The debts of history;
The temples of a vanished sect
  Have crumbled in the sea.

The god has nothing left to hide
  And nothing left to show:
To him alone will he confide
  Who's learned himself to know.

334.

16 Dec. 2022

Not long now 'til ChatGPT
  Can handle complex metres:
Its Golden Age of poesy
  Just needs some robot readers.

The Hub ran a series of interesting articles about the phenomenon of AI in December 2022.

335.

4 May 2022

Yes, balance: Cut the word in stone.
  Past, future; blindness, sight;
Injustice, justice; metal, bone;
  The darkness and the light.

In evil rise, arise in good;
  Be chosen, boy, and thus
Unlearn what had been understood;
  Be born, be fatherless.

Betrayer slain, slayer betrayed,
  The constellations tend
Toward the final fate you made –
  To balance in the end.

To Anakin Skywalker on May the Fourth, a day of celebration for the Star Wars fandom.

336.

22 May 2023

Victoria Day 2023.

Whether beneath the Roman yoke,
  The Persian or the Han,
The longhouse of the Fivefold Folk,
  The hooves of the Great Khan,

Or now, when everyone expounds
  He never was so free
(Until he stumbles out of bounds
  And learns conformity),

The price of peace is ever steep:
  That we must smile and kneel
To distant emperors, like sheep
  That thank the shepherd's zeal.

May every empire be so bland,
  So cheerful in its aim
As hers, who ruled this happy land
  Before the Yankee came.

337.

1 July 2023

Dominion Day 2023.

Land of the maple and the fir,
  Land of the cedar tree,
Land of the ice, where few folk stir
  Along the grinding sea;

Land of the grass, of lakes, of pools
  Where cruel mosquitoes grow,
Land of the western rain that cools
  The mountain with its snow;

Here we were born, or here we came,
  Here we shall build anew
Fair cities under that fair name
  And to that name be true.

The task, of course, is vast, so vast
  Some falter or despair:
But courage, friends, we'll win at last
  A mighty land to share.

338.

11 Nov. 2021

Remembrance Day 2021.

They lie here still, the good, the bad,
  The most brave and the least,
The ever-joyful and the sad,
  For Canada deceased.

And here the lucky too lie dead,
  Shelled in the lung, the neck,
Shot in the leg or chest or head,
  Unlucky for a sec.

Quiet together let them lie
  Always in this the same,
That, though all men, once born, must die,
  Few get a deathless name;

And only at their chiseled grave
  A people kneels to vow
To be as good or great or brave
  As luck and peace allow.

339.

11 Nov. 2022

Remembrance Day 2022.

In fields long free of pits and wire,
  In peace at last they rest;
What God and King too oft require
  They gave — our dead, our best;

Today in memory they appear,
  An undiminished host:
Still, if we listen, we can hear
  Their Last, eternal Post.

340.

11 Nov. 2023

Remembrance Day 2023.

Today we are not here: the breath
  Of history blows today,
Sweeping us to the scene of death
  So very far away.

Just listen: now no noises mar
  The silence as we tread
These dusty rocks of Kandahar
  On which our soldiers bled.

Here is the snow that falls so pure
  Along Ortona's lanes,
'Til soon in its bright quilt occur
  So many bloody stains.

Here lastly is the liquid mud
  Of Flanders and of France;
That echo is the distant thud
  That heralds our advance.

In rock, in snow, in mud we greet
  Those dead on our behalf;
They lie beneath our very feet,
  The world their cenotaph.

341.

10 Nov. 2024

Remembrance Day 2024.

At Vimy and at Passchendaele,
To bullet, shell, and bomb,
At Ypres, where they dared not fail,
They fell, and at the Somme;

And at Dieppe, in Italy,
And over Juno's sand,
Then down the roads of Normandy;
And there the crosses stand,

Immortal as the flowers indeed
Blossoming every May,
Red in their petals, black in seed,
That mark Remembrance Day:

As we remember those who died,
And as Last Post sounds clear,
Forgive me if I turn aside
To shed a private tear.

342.

29 Nov. 2021

Hanukkah 2021.

The tyrant's army held the town,
  The temple lay profaned;
The days of honour and renown
  Had well and truly waned.

But in the mountains Judas raised
  The Hammer of the Lord,
And as the people watched, amazed,
  He smashed the tyrant's sword.

Jerusalem is taken back,
  The righteous man is king;
But who can find, amid the wrack,
  A righteous offering?

Fear not: for eight full days and nights
  We watched, astonished, awed
To learn we'll never lack the lights
  To glorify our God.

343.

31 Dec. 2021

2021, the second year of Covid, was miserable for everyone.

Adieu, two thousand twenty-one,
  Your party won't be missed:
If that was your idea of fun,
  Just leave me off the list.

344.

30 Dec. 2022

Year-in-review, 2022.

So, 2022, farewell!
  The currency inflated.
People no longer look like hell.
  Hysteria abated.

The Russians rolled in, got rolled back.
  The poor locked-down Chinese
Might well, or might well not, attack.
  Europe's about to freeze.

Justin and Joe are still half-here.
  The Jays somehow screwed up.
Lord Musk now rules the Twittersphere,
  And Messi won the Cup.

It's fair to say my Muse is thriving:
  I wrote a thousand rhymes;
Amidst the shrieking and the striving,
  I'm grateful for good times.

345.

30 Dec. 2023

Year-in-review, 2023.

At last the crazy T-bar ride
  Of 2023
Is worth it, for the fireside
  And week of après-ski;

The bear's asleep inside his den,
  The trucker's reached his stop,
The reverend's said his last amen,
  The elves have locked the shop.

Here there's no cant, no demagogue,
  But many a tasty morsel,
The Santa hat, the endless nog,
  And snowshoes at the doorsill:

However warm, however snug,
  Let's head off out the door
And earn that first hot chocolate mug
  Of 2024.

BOOK V

Lyrical Poems

346.

3 Feb. 2024

Noah and the dove.

Do you not know me? I'm your dove,
  Yours was the gentle hand
That launched me to the world above
  To seek a lost green land;

More massive than the human mind
  Can reckon rolls the sea,
The end of it was hard to find:
  A lonely olive tree.

Far to the north it lies, and there
  The air of heaven blowing
Brushes the grass, the flowers fair,
  An islet ever growing.

Yet back I flew, until all things
  Grew dim, and grey, and dreary,
Until my white, once mighty wings
  Were infinitely weary,

Bearing me o'er the ceaseless foam:
  Some god had willed it so;
But faith in you has borne me home
  These few leaves to bestow.

347.

15 July 2023

David and Goliath.

Just point me at the Philistines
And hand me what I need;
Look how they're dancing in their lines,
Not knowing how they'll bleed:

The chariots of Ashkelon,
The champion of Gath
Have seen, my friends, their final dawn,
A dawn, my friends, of wrath;

Oh, let him curse me by his gods,
The gods of that foul horde:
Am I a prisoner of the odds
Who fear none but the Lord?

A boy, they say? Go tell the king
That with a single stone
I'll make his courtly annals ring
And win this war alone.

348.

14 Dec. 2021

They say we're getting wooden swords —
  The emperor's own decree;
I guess the bloodsport ill accords
  With his philosophy;

From now on skill shall be displayed,
  And not our guts and brains;
No reason now to be afraid,
  Or so the man maintains.

Maybe it's time to go back home
  And find a country grave;
'Cause what's the point of life in Rome
  If Rome won't know I'm brave?

The emperor Marcus Aurelius insisted that Roman gladiators use wooden swords in combat rather than sharp swords.

349.

29 July 2023

Horatian ode.

Don't try and count the stars, refrain
  From measuring out the sea:
It's rash indeed to let the brain
  Defy infinity.

So too the years since Caesar fought
  To break and conquer Gaul
Extend beyond the reach of thought:
  They make our lives too small.

Trim back your appetites: the day
  Is short enough: there's room
In every schedule, Elsa Mae,
  For sunshine ere the gloom:

Here is a ballfield, here's the crack
  Of ball and maple bat,
The catch, the runner racing back,
  And nearly out at that.

350.

21 Oct. 2023

Looking forward to the 2023 World Series.

I liked that politician's style:
  He's all about the deed;
But it's been clear for quite a while
  He's just another screed.

They said, Try this philosopher,
  He quotes the saints of yore;
I found his vision all too pure:
  Perfection is a bore.

To Science finally I turned,
  All the clear proofs she's shown;
And so by patient study learned
  How little can be known.

Life is too precious for that stuff,
  For paragraphs and theories:
Life teaches that it's quite enough
  To catch the World Series.

351.

23 Sept.
2023

Just as a droplet-dripping mist
  Of Newfoundland will coil
The lowering sky into a fist,
  Then down the valley toil

To reach each cot, unless tucked tight,
  So sickness picks its way
By each degree of Fahrenheit
  Until the dusk holds sway.

Lie back and think of distant fields
  Kissed to a blush of flowers,
The wicker picnic that she wields,
  The pleasantest of hours;

And in her hand a merry book,
  And in the book a poem,
A truth you never quite forsook,
  Reminding you of home:

A place no mist can ever reach,
  A place the sun's too bright,
Too beautiful for human speech,
  Above the realm of night.

352.

13 Jan. 2024

After Pope's *Ode on Solitude.*

Happy the man who lives unplugged,
Reading a favourite book,
Who warms with logs that he has lugged
Some modest off-grid nook;

His woolen blankets, quite untaxed,
Suffice against the chill;
He rises eager, sleeps relaxed
And very seldom ill.

Not in hot rages at the wheel
His lifespan burns away:
Rather he hears one snowmobile,
If even that, per day.

No screen, however huge or small,
Cramps his attention span;
No streaming services enthrall
A free, free-minded man.

Thus let me live, unseen, unchafed,
Snug with my kids and wife,
What now is to so few vouchsafed:
A happy, quiet life.

353.

8 July 2023

Spring in Halifax.

Better than temples, far from thieves,
  This oracle can speak
Truth in the fluttering of the leaves,
  Truth in a branch's creak.

The question is the same today
  As when, in youth, I came
To ask him if—well, anyway,
  My footstep is the same.

Look to the answer of the birds,
  Ascending from the right:
A fool prefers a scheme of words
  To their delightful flight

Across the air, across a lake
  So crystal-bright I blink;
Descending like one fresh awake,
  From that bright lake I drink,

Then raise my palms in ancient prayer,
  Palms high against the sky:
The god has put my answer there:
  The god can never die.

354.

5 Aug. 2023

The mountain grizzly.

High in the Selkirks, where it's sweet
  To spend a summer's day
In feasting on the berries' meat,
  A grizzly picks his way:

He little notes the rising light
  Upon Sir Donald's peak:
Uninterested in such a sight
  With berries still to seek.

But in your body beats a soul
  Pointed by God to beauty,
Beauty that makes the spirit whole,
  Along with love of duty:

The race of Man can never roam
  Or wander without end;
We bring our tales of beauty home
  To share it with a friend,

How by the glacier, far aloft,
  Where the great eagles soar,
We trod the moss as soft as soft
  And saw the grizzly roar.

355.

27 Aug. 2021

Where beavers build, where tall moose roam,
  Where boulders edge the lake:
That land of silver birch is home;
  I travel for its sake.

Peacefully where the deathless stream
  Its crystal currant spills,
I'll raise my hut; 'til then I'll dream
  Of distant northern hills.

Adapted from "Land of the Silver Birch," attributed to Pauline Johnson.

356.

4 Sept. 2021

Tonight I'm slender as a loon
  Calling a distant mate
With my three notes, my lonely tune:
  "Just here, my love, I wait."

Tonight the forest looms in me
  Untraveled; what can stir
The white pine's lofty dignity,
  The secrets of the fir?

Tonight we'll shed the skin of man,
  Our love and dread of men;
Here it begins where it began:
  We sit with gods again.

Summer night on the Canadian Shield.

357.

4 June 2021

I wish I were the wind and you
Were walking in the sun,
So I might brush you as I blew
And ’round your shoulders run.

Adapted from the Greek Anthology 5.83: Εἴθ’ ἄνεμος γενόμην, σὺ δ’ ἐπιστείχουσα παρ’ αὐγὰς / στήθεα γυμνώσαις, καί με πνέοντα λάβοις.

358.

26 Aug. 2023

Sinuous pillar of the wood,
I’ve wondered oftentimes
If many a slender birch has stood
Where your white marble climbs;

Now evermore the rich dirt mounts,
And there the saplings tremble,
Fresh entries in the earth’s accounts,
Which rain and spring assemble.

Eternal lake, a glacier’s deed,
Mirror of dusky skies,
Cradle of the pike-haunted reed,
The loon’s late-summer cries

Summon his kindred from your bays
To seek a distant coast
With notes beyond mere mortal praise,
And those I’ll miss the most

When someday I’ll be nature’s nurse,
Returned to clay and loam,
Or maybe distant skies traverse
To reach another home.

359.

2 Setp. 2023

Inner-tubing on the lake.

A tube is all I need, a rope,
  Some gas, my trusty brother,
An engine and a frothy slope
  Of water, now another,

Ripping the pure, once-peaceful bay
  In death-defying bliss,
Until my grip or his gives way,
  Then out into th' abyss

Of crystal lake, the dazzling light,
  The taste of forest brooks,
My dad's voice calling from the right,
  My brother's hand that hooks

Me on once more. The engine roars,
  The vast horsepower sings;
This kingdom of the great outdoors
  Has picked a pair of kings.

360.

12 Jan. 2023

The summer foreseen from the winter.

Someday, relieved of obligations,
  I'll read books all day long,
At sunset pour out bright libations,
  Hearing the loon's clear song;

I'll bid the stars good night, crawl in,
  Sleep soundly 'til I wake,
Then happily again begin
  A June day at the Lake.

361.

18 Nov. 2023

The air is cool, the light is grim:
  Already winter's hand
Has brushed my leaves from every limb
  Yet still I think I'll stand

Another year, another age:
  My roots are never broken;
There was, you see, an ancient sage
  Who planted me, a token

Of some profound, forgotten truth;
  Around me all the stones
Have fallen, torn by time's sharp tooth;
  Through them the cold wind moans;

But every spring my branches sway,
  With yellow blossom gilt,
In hopes he may return some day,
  His oracle rebuilt.

Are you the sage? Shall you restore
  What people most revere?
If not, that's fine, for one year more
  I don't mind waiting here.

362.

20 Jan. 2024

On philology.

Here is the forest of old words,
  And none may enter in
Unless he reads the flight of birds
  For what will be, has been.

The roots go deep, the branches twist,
  The seedlings fight for light
Amid the universal mist
  That cloaks the Druid's rite:

Here Bentley and Chantraine unlocked
  The secrets of the Greek;
Here like an elf-lord Tolkien walked
  And taught the trees to speak.

Philology in youth I breathed,
  Again I wish I could:
But I must pass by, hatchet sheathed,
  Nor dare to cut the wood.

363.

22 July 2023

The library, the city's heart,
   Once stood here, long forlorn
Before the city fell apart,
   Before the books were torn

And scattered, rotting leaf by leaf:
   A fragmentary poem
Speaks of the passing poet's grief
   On meeting some dead tome.

Here Shakespeare's works once sat, complete;
   Here every orphaned name,
Tannyson, Hubert, Audens, Keat,
   Had readers, not mere fame;

Perhaps in some untouched hard drive,
   Defying time's decay,
The Sonnets may be found alive
   And bless our latter day.

364.

16 Dec. 2023

It took a lot of blood and pain,
  A lot of fractious Franks
To pave the way for Charlemagne;
  And yet they get no thanks,

For history overlooks the toil
  Of ordinary men,
The battles with the rocky soil,
  Until the moment when

A people booms, its cities blessed
  As arts and commerce thrive;
'Til then, to see them, who'd have guessed?
  The lesson is: survive,

Survive the droughts, survive the cults,
  Survive the philistines,
Cast off the lust for quick results:
  We'll scan the sky for signs

The dream of glory isn't dead:
  I hear a distant drum:
Our glory waits some way ahead
  In what we will become.

365.

24 Feb. 2024

This man is learnèd in the law:
  That's super, I suppose;
Unless he's got the fatal flaw
  That law is all he knows.

This lad's no prisoner of fun,
  They've trained him to obey:
That's great, unless he gets a gun
  And marches up my way.

This woman is so pure of heart,
  So pious and so good,
She's gone and ripped the king apart
  Deep in the sacred wood.

When virtue's limited, it seems
  There's nothing more propitious;
But nothing's perfect in extremes:
  Excess makes virtue vicious.

366.

16 March 2023

Take off your toque: the breeze is soft,
  And like a mother's hand
It brushes winter cares aloft
  To some far distant land.

Soon, soon the secret sap will rise,
  The hungry bear awake,
The ice quite suddenly devise
  An exit from the lake;

Now let the country breathe again
  After its winter: come,
Forgive the many sins of men,
  The breeze is gentle: strum

The chords of summer: sing that tune
  That everybody knows;
For, even as we sing, too soon
  The wind of autumn blows.

367.

27 Apr. 2023

One rule this old world turns upon:
  What can't last, Luke, will not;
Though water, fire, and air go on,
  The way of earth is rot;

And what will rot, alas, first wilts,
  And what will wilt first sags:
The statues topple, palace tilts,
  The pharaoh robed in rags.

But though I vanish and my name
  Live not for evermore,
My soul's quick atoms stay the same;
  And who knows what's in store?

Perhaps, like Socrates, I'll meet
  Hesiod, Homer too,
Whose songs from his eternal seat
  Still make this old world new.

368.

1 June 2024

For Kevin Lynch.

Of course I'll never abdicate
  My duty; yet the air
Lures me beyond the daily hate
  Along a coastland fair,

Where fog and meadow, rock and sea
  Infinitely combine;
With violent eternity
  I peacefully align.

Aye, let the vast Atlantic rage
  And find I'm still the same;
For true philosophies assuage
  The will to praise and blame.

These are the Isles of the Blest
  By antique poets sung:
Here someday I'll forever rest,
  The salt upon my tongue.

369.

21 Sept. 2024

Ode to Bacteria.

With grandeur? No, the world is charged
  With writhing detail, whence
Few things are ever much enlarged,
  The dawn, the voice immense

Of mountain storm that strikes us dumb;
  A vaster nature lurks,
The world of the bacterium,
  And there God mostly works:

For these He made when He was young,
  Not on a passing whim,
Nonillions still unseen, unsung
  Except to Him, by Him;

Man is the planet's tireless rover,
  Half-bard, half-scientist,
But when Man's foolish time is over,
  They're destined to persist.

370.

24 Aug. 2024

The soft crescendo of the light,
  The glimmer of the lawn,
The latest triumph over night:
  These are the gifts of dawn.

Oh, let the sleepy people scoff,
  Poor prisoners of the lamp;
A bite of breakfast and we're off
  To stretch and breathe and tramp

Up and along the seaside ridge,
  Down to a secret beach,
Then onward to a little bridge
  Until at last we reach

A pillar, stark against the east,
  Too sombre to discuss,
A work of those long since deceased,
  Known only now to us.

371.

28 Sept. 2024

So where's Napoleon now? Such fame
  The world had never known;
Today he's little but a name,
  The details overthrown.

With him whole nations dreamt of glory,
  Making Europe shake;
But in the end the hero's story
  Finishes as we wake:

The drums of death and destiny
  Roll onward and away:
All triumph, all catastrophe
  Fades to a distant grey,

Except in history: history's call
  No poet can refuse;
Today Napoleon owes it all
  To somebody's soft Muse.

372.

20 July 2024

Ode to Fatigue.

When the last patch of lawn is mown,
  When Christmas dinner's done,
When the last perfect fastball's thrown,
  And when the campaign's won,

To thee in gratitude we turn,
  With thee, Fatigue, we slouch;
And though for Sleep we say we yearn
  In fact we want a couch,

A couch on which to take a drop,
  And talk, and be admired;
For dull soft Sleep what fool would swap
  The bliss of being tired?

I'll savour heavy lids, the ache
  That proves the day well spent;
What else besides Fatigue can make
  A body so content?

And when, against my will, I rise,
  I'll seek thee through the day,
Thee whom the lazy demonize,
  Goddess of work and play.

373.

3 Aug. 2024

Lift up your world-weary eye
  And gaze on what is great:
No cant pollutes the bright night sky:
  There history has no weight.

The slander and the jealousy
  Of all-too-human cares
Is nothing to infinity;
  Our curses and our prayers,

Our loves and tears, our heartfelt needs,
  Our injuries thin-skinned,
Are less than dandelion seeds
  Blown low along the wind.

Remember something lofty, Matt,
  Hides in this skin of ours:
It makes us both go quiet at
  The silence of the stars.

374.

7 Sept. 2024

You fear that Greece will be forgotten
  And darkness fill the land,
Zeus's great oak at last prove rotten,
  His statue sunk in sand;

That sheep will roam where Alexander
  Sat on the royal throne
And some barbarian commander
  New rituals intone.

Fear not: the glory of the past
  No century makes less,
Too bright, too lofty, and too vast
  For us to curse or bless.

Fear this instead: that we may be
  Forgotten by the Greeks,
Mere notes to their long history,
  Mere notes no reader seeks.

375.

6 July 2024

Infinite summer, endless breeze
  That makes the birch leaves sing,
Delicate gentle daiquiris,
  The hummingbird's loud wing,

Lake sword of the eternal sun
  Across the ripples bright,
In which all swimmers swim as one,
  Fluid in their delight;

These happy things can't last forever,
  For happiness depends
On knowing how the seasons sever
  Our wishes from their ends;

And if Calypso tempted me
  With endless perfect life,
I'd also choose mortality,
  My island, and my wife.

376.

Unpublished

You're back, book? Oh, is that a smirk?
  You've got your leaf, some bark;
You're just in time: I'm hard at work
  Building a better Ark.

Noah and the dove.